This book and all other Destiny Image, Revival Press, and Treasure House books are available at Christian bookstores and distributors worldwide.

For a U.S. bookstore nearest you, call **1-800-722-6774**.
For more information on foreign distributors,
call **717-532-3040**.
Or reach us on the Internet: **http://www.reapernet.com**

CRASHING SATAN'S PARTY

Destroying the Works
of the Adversary
in Your Life

Dr. Millicent Thompson

Treasure House
An Imprint of
Destiny Image® Publishers, Inc.
P.O. Box 310
Shippensburg, PA 17257-0310

"For where your treasure is,
there will your heart be also." Matthew 6:21

ISBN 1-56043-268-3

For Worldwide Distribution
Printed in the U.S.A.

Third Printing: 1997   Fourth Printing: 1998

This book and all other Destiny Image, Revival Press,
and Treasure House books are available at Christian bookstores
and distributors worldwide.

For a U.S. bookstore nearest you, call **1-800-722-6774**.
For more information on foreign distributors, call **717-532-3040**.
Or reach us on the Internet: **http://www.reapernet.com**

DEDICATION

This book is dedicated to the two "joys" of my life, Jason and Melissa. Thank you for sharing Mommy—again.

ACKNOWLEDGMENT

This book has been very well-received around the world. I extend my sincere thanks to Reverend Linda Pratt, Executive Director of Millicent Thompson Ministries, for her time, commitment, and professionalism in the preparation of this book. Thank you Baptist Worship Center church family for your obedience to the will of God and your continued support of your Pastor. I pray God's richest blessings upon you.

ENDORSEMENTS

"Dr. Millicent Thompson is a valuable and viable voice that speaks to the Body of Christ in a practical and yet unique way. Her years of experience provide us with insightful exposure of the onslaught of the enemy. Again, she inspires us to become fortified and empowered in our Christian walk."

Bishop Barbara M. Amos
Faith Deliverance Christian Center
Norfolk, VA

"Harnessing the power of the Word of God, combined with the reality of personal experience, Dr. Millicent Thompson's preaching, teaching, and writing elevate us to new levels in Christ. She is indeed a fresh voice for the time in which we live."

Bishop Donald Hilliard
The Cathedral-Second Baptist Church
Perth Amboy, NJ

"Genuine, committed, a seeker of excellence! In this book Dr. Millicent Thompson offers a theology of liberation. This liberation will direct the reader to the inevitability of success and peace."

Bishop Richard Moore
Holy Unity Baptist Church
Jamaica, NY

"Dr. Millicent Thompson is a dynamic pastor, preacher, author, and conference speaker. It is through her many years of ministry that she awakens the reader to the reality that turning to God is our best source of strength."

Bishop Alfred A. Owens, Jr.
Greater Mt. Calvary Holy Church
Washington, DC

CONTENTS

INTRODUCTION

This book is about the victimization suffered by every child of God who does not know and understand the strategies and tactics of satan. Ignorance is the devil's playground. Satan, along with his cohorts, is not as blatant as many believe. He is subtle and delights in deception. He is shrewd, cunning, and crafty in his operations.

The prophet Hosea warned the Hebrews when he said that God's people are destroyed for a lack of knowledge (see Hos. 4:6). This book exposes satan's method of operation.

Many have unfairly attributed acts of the devil to God. The results have been devastating. We must be able to recognize *who* is doing *what* in our lives and react correctly according to God's Word. We determine whether or not the devil can operate in our life.

Some of us would like to attribute our spiritual problems to these *last and evil days* or to negative influences. However, we must be more specific than that. Our adversary has a name, personality, personal attributes, and a specific method of operation. When we as members of the Body of Christ are unaware of satan's strategies, we become ready prey for every subtle and overt attack. Satan rejoices over every downfall. He celebrates and all hell is happy when they hinder the power of God in our life.

This book will bring clarity and understanding to every scheme, scam, plot, and plan that satan uses against us. We must do our part if we are to be overcomers. We need to take positive action. God's Word thunders down through the ages with a solution for every one of satan's offenses. We must know what the Bible reveals to us about the character and attributes of the devil. With this knowledge, we can *crash* his party. We can *destroy* the works of the adversary.

I've met the enemy! I have looked him and his demons square in the face and crashed his party. I have become an expert in dealing with the enemy. I learned how to take authority over him and use the power God has given me. I know what it means to be an overcomer. I have put what I have learned from God's Word into practice in my life. Satan still exercises great power in the world, but his final destiny is assured. The final crashing will take place when Christ puts down all rebellion in the earth. Satan's season of celebration has ended. The party's over.

As you understand satan's method of operation, the difficulties you experience as a Christian will have greater meaning. Not only will you learn how the enemy operates, but you will learn how to resist him. God will stir up and stimulate your gift of discernment.

God has burned this message into my heart. I believe the Holy Spirit will use this book to bring great liberty to your life and ministry.

Rev. Dr. Millicent Thompson
Pastor, The Baptist Worship Center

Chapter 1

AN OPEN INVITATION

*Be sober, be vigilant; because your adversary
the devil, as a roaring lion, walketh about,
seeking whom he may devour.*
1 Peter 5:8

"*I*N THE *name of Jesus*," I shouted, "*I command you to get out of my house, my home life, and my ministry. Go back to hell where you be-long!*" My voice quivered and my knees trembled. Yet, to my amazement, every demon spirit residing in my home left. In the spirit realm I saw them packing their bags, loading their gear, and rushing toward my front door in a feverish attempt to flee the power of God. Taking authority over demons was new to me, and to my delight, it worked!

I was saved, sanctified, and filled with the Holy Spirit, but I still experienced attacks of the enemy. They came on every level at different times in my life. Like most born-again believers, I knew how to love God. I knew who Jesus was and how to build my relationship with Him. However, I was still totally ignorant about the devil. My understanding of satan was basic and limited at best. I knew he was wicked and had rebelled against God. Yet, I did not know about his plan to bring down the Kingdom of God in the life of every believer; nor did I know that my adversary had a name, personality, personal attributes, and a specific method of operation in the lives of Christians. I was ready prey—a sitting duck—because of my own ignorance.

Like most Christians, popular teachings had lulled me to sleep, convincing me that God's hedge of protection was impenetrable. I felt safe, secure, and protected. Then, like an iron chariot, satan came crashing into my comfortable Christian life and left signs of destruction everywhere.

I cried out to God many times in the middle of the night, *"Where are You? Why aren't You rescuing me? When are You going to help me?"* I *expected* God to help me. I did not realize that He wanted to *teach* me how to help myself. He had already given me all the power I needed.

Satan Throws Surprise Parties

Satan does not have the power to rob us of our salvation. Jesus assures us that no one can pluck or snatch us out of God's hand.

> *My sheep hear My voice, and I know them, and they follow Me: And I give unto them eternal life; and they shall never perish, neither shall any man pluck them out of My hand* (John 10:27-28).

Just as a shepherd protects his sheep, Jesus protects His people from eternal harm. Although believers can expect to suffer on earth, satan cannot harm our souls or take away our eternal life with God. However, satan can, with God's approval, cause suffering. If we do not deal with suffering properly, it will weaken our faith and trust in God.

Earth is satan's domain. God has given him limited power to reign on this earth for a time. Children of God are not immune from attacks of satan. Every believer will face trials in this life.

We must understand that these trials can bring glory to God. He can bring good out of any bad situation. When trouble comes we should not waste time grumbling and complaining. We need to spend time learning how to combat the enemy. The Word of God gives us insight, tools, and strategies to combat satan's attacks. If we use them, every problem will become an opportunity to enlarge our faith and honor God.

Just as satan beguiled Adam and Eve in the garden, he beguiles us with his subtleness and perverted deception. He and his demonic cohorts are not as blatant as many believe. He is subtle and delights in deception. His operations are cunning, crafty, and shrewd.

Quite often his attacks surprise us. In fact, we may not recognize his presence until his plan of destruction is well under way. Ignorance is the devil's playground and can make us an unwilling victim. We need to understand and anticipate his tactics. The prophet Hosea warned, "My people are destroyed for lack of knowledge..." (Hos. 4:6).

Satan Still Says "Come"

As a pastor, I have often watched new Christians become discouraged because they mistakenly thought their new found faith made them immune to satanic attack. They believed they no longer needed to worry about the old habits and sins that had nearly destroyed their life. The truth is quite to the contrary!

When we accept Jesus Christ as Lord and Savior, we are no longer servants of sin. Paul said in Romans 6:6-7:

Knowing this, that our old man is crucified with Him, that the body of sin might be destroyed, that henceforth we should not serve sin. For he that is dead is freed from sin.

However, we must remember that we live in a fallen world. The battle between good and evil still rages on. Yes, even to the believer, satan still says "come." He reminds us of our faults, attacks our emotions, and tempts us through fleshly desires. Satan will tell us that we are defeated when we do something wrong. He tries to convince us that the works of satan will always reign in us because our flesh is weak.

I am reminded of a young man in my congregation who struggles with a serious alcohol problem. His addiction began in his early teen years, and it has all but destroyed his life through chronic unemployment, homelessness, crime, frequent hospitalizations, and a general feeling of hopelessness. My heart aches every time I pray with him and watch his eyes fill with tears as together we ask God to free him from this demon called alcoholism. He loves the Lord and cannot understand why satan is still trying to destroy his life. He once asked me during a counseling session, "Why doesn't the devil leave me alone? I thought that once I decided to come to Jesus these old problems would leave me." I quickly reminded him that satan's goal is to bring down the Kingdom of God in the life of every believer.

Carnality opens the door for the schemes or wiles of satan (see Eph. 6:11) to divert, and in some cases destroy, our witness. Satan's wiles are cunning devices he uses with expert accuracy. The power of our flesh is no real match for the devil. Our warfare against him must be waged with spiritual weapons so that we can stand against principalities, powers, the rulers of the darkness of this world, and spiritual wickedness in high places (see Eph. 6:12). We cannot crash satan's party until we identify the ways he works in our lives. We must know his weapons, as well as the weapons given to us by the Spirit of God (see Eph. 6:10-18). For instance, to use the shield of faith (see Eph. 6:10) we must identify the direction from which the evil darts come toward us.

I tell the new Christians in my church that when you accept the Lord satan does not cancel his plans for your life. In fact, he accelerates his plan; as a believer you are a greater threat to his kingdom. I encourage new believers, like that young man with the alcohol problem, that the power of God is always with the believer. Jesus said we would experience tribulation in this life but we are to be encouraged. We are to be of good cheer. He overcame this world and because He lives in us we too shall overcome (see Jn. 16:33). As I give that young man a tissue to wipe his eyes, I tell him, "We play a critical part in the battles we win against satan."

Paul offers us some practical advice:

...present your bodies a living sacrifice, holy, acceptable unto God, which is your reasonable service. And be not conformed to this world: but be ye transformed by the renewing of your mind, that ye may prove what is that good, and acceptable, and perfect, will of God (Romans 12:1-2).

Have you let the devil pull you into some areas where you know you will be defeated?

Paul cried out, "O wretched man that I am! The things that the spirit does not want to do, I find myself doing. The things

I should do, I never accomplish. The devil has me in this battle, and I will never be able to win" (see Rom. 7:19-20,24). Yet Paul began to lift his eyes to another arena when he said, "Thanks be to God, I find my victory in Him" (see Rom. 7:25).

Satan cunningly dwells in areas where he can turn fleshly desires in the wrong direction. Christians must recognize his enticement and say, "This body is the temple of the Holy Spirit, and God can use it to manifest His glory and love. I will not partake of the corruption the world produces."

But Why Me?

If God is a good God, why do I have to suffer? I commit- ted my life to the Lord and things got worse, not better. Why do bad things happen to good people? Why doesn't God just tell satan to "back off"? I feel like a target.

Many believers have asked these questions over and over. They encounter one trial after another, just like Job did. (See Job 1–2.) Job, a righteous man who had been greatly blessed by God, was a perfect target for satan.

Satan had to ask God for permission to take Job's wealth, children, and health away. God limited satan's authority. He could not and still cannot exceed the limits that God sets (see Job 1:12). Satan attempted to drive a wedge between Job and God by getting Job to believe God's governing of the world was unjust.

As we read about the calamity and suffering of Job, we must remember that we live in a fallen world where good behavior is not always rewarded, and bad behavior is not al- ways punished. When we see a notorious criminal prosper- ing or an innocent child in pain, we say *"That is wrong!"* Yes, it is. Sin has twisted justice and has made our world un- predictable and ugly.

The Book of Job shows a good man suffering for no apparent reason. Sadly, our world is like that. But Job's story does not end in despair. Through Job's life we can see that faith in God is justified even when our situations look hopeless.

Faith based upon rewards or prosperity is hollow. *Unshakable faith* must be built on the confidence that God knows what He is doing and that His ultimate purpose will come to pass. God is all-wise and all-powerful. His will is perfect, yet He does not always act in ways that we understand.

Any person who is committed to God can expect satan's attacks. Satan hates God, and God's people as well. We are not exempt from trouble just because we love God. Although we may not be able to fully understand the pain we experience, our pain can lead us to rediscover God.

Special Targets

When we suffer, we must not conclude that God has abandoned us. He did not abandon Job. Sometimes believers may actually suffer more than unbelievers; they become satan's special targets. We must be willing to trust God in spite of unanswered questions. If we always know *why* we suffer, our faith will not have any room to grow.

Satan cannot move without God's permission. God's power also resides in God's people and can be used to overcome these attacks. Knowing this should cause us to remain close to the One who is greater than satan—God Himself.

Blaming God

Satan and his evil forces are the agents of this destruction, not God. The only sense in which God participates in it is through withholding His protection and delivering the individual over to the devil for His divine purpose. The Book of Job plainly demonstrates this truth. Who destroyed Job's family and possessions and then afflicted Job's body? The answer is "satan." Who gave permission for this to take place? The answer is "God." (See Job 1:12-19; 2:7.)

This is, and always will be, the case in instances of affliction and destruction. God gives permission, but satan causes the actual occurrence of accidents, sickness, disease, and calamity. Then he persuades mankind to think God has brought these things to pass. Thus God is erroneously *blamed* by millions for the work of the devil, even by Christians who should know better. If we do not understand that satan is the initiator and propagator of all wicked and evil things, a spirit of bitterness and anger against God can easily take root in us.

God merely grants His permission and uses evil to work for the good of the righteous. Early in my ministry I remember visiting a parishioner who was in the hospital recovering from a stroke. The stroke had left him severely handicapped and almost unable to speak. I was excited about visiting this man. He was a long-standing member of our church (I had known him since my childhood), and everyone admired him for his commitment and enthusiasm for the Church and for God. I knew he would talk about "the goodness of Jesus and all that He's done for me" as he always did.

From the time that I arrived at his room, until the visit ended one hour later, I felt captive, like a prisoner. Despite his slurred speech, this good deacon and committed pillar of the church railed against God and spewed out his anger against God for *causing* his illness.

I have run across this quite often throughout my ministry— Christians blaming God for sickness, death, divorce, mental illness, crime, war, and all manner of evil. Satan must be having a good laugh.

God's permission is not the same as performing the destructive work of satan. Withdrawing protection and allowing another to destroy is not the same as doing the destruction. God delivers. Satan destroys.

Satan's Plan, God's Purpose

Satan plans destruction and ruin in the life of every believer. He wants to sabotage our good works, nullify our testimony, and bring waste to every good deed that brings glory to God. God's purpose, however, is to build an intimate relationship with each one of us and teach us how to destroy the works of the adversary. God will use any means necessary to draw us closer to Him. Therefore, He allows satan to continue his relentless assaults in order to:

1. Develop character and faith in the believer (see Jas. 1:12; 1 Pet. 1:7-13; 5:8-9; 2 Pet. 1:4-9; Jude 20-24).
2. Keep the believer humble (see 2 Cor. 12:7).
3. Provide conflict for the saints so that they may be rewarded through overcoming (see 1 Jn. 2:13; 4:1-6; Rev. 2:7,11,17,26-28; 3:5,12,21).
4. Demonstrate the power of God over the power of satan (see Mk. 16:17-20; 2 Cor. 4:9; Eph. 2:7; 3:10).
5. Afflict people in order to bring them to repentance (see 1 Cor. 5:1-7; 2 Cor. 2:5-11; Job 33:14-30).
6. Purge man of all possibilities of falling in the eternal future (see Rev. 21).

On-the-Job Training

I almost perished at the hands of the enemy simply because of my lack of understanding. Satan tried to destroy me, but God wanted to teach me how to become an *overcomer*. He gave me an opportunity to receive some on-the-job training (personal experience) in spiritual warfare.

Was I prepared for the test? Yes! Did I need such knowledge? Yes! Christians who are serious about their walk and work for the Lord will encounter satan along the way. Therefore, we must be equipped with the knowledge to overcome him. Knowledge is understanding gained through experience or study. Understanding what is true, right, or lasting is wisdom, and true wisdom comes from God. God is more than willing to pour out His wisdom to us (see Jas. 1:5).

Satan is *your* adversary too. He is seeking to devour you. Right now he is either devising or carrying out a plan designed to cause your destruction. If successful, he will rejoice at your downfall. Nevertheless, you can take the wind out of his sails and dismantle every one of his wicked plans and devices. Open your heart and spirit as you pray this prayer with me:

Lord, pour out Your knowledge and wisdom upon me. Help me to see who satan is and how he works. I do not want to be his helpless victim. Teach me how to overcome him. Guide me through Your Word, and speak to me in prayer. Amen.

Chapter 2

THE DEVIL'S PLAYGROUND

Let this mind be in you, which was also in Christ Jesus:
who, being in the form of God, thought it not robbery
to be equal with God.
Philippians 2:5-6

THE HUMAN mind is the devil's playground. Here, satan wreaks havoc in the life of every unwitting, unsuspecting believer. The Christian's behavior is not his *primary* target. Instead, satan targets the human mind, for he knows that if he can influence your mind with wicked thoughts, those thoughts will eventually affect your behavior.

Mind Games

Paul calls satan "the god of this world" and explains that his work is to deceive. Satan also blinds the minds of the unbelievers to keep them from seeing the light of the gospel of Jesus Christ.

In whom the god of this world hath blinded the minds of them which believe not, lest the light of the glorious gospel of Christ, who is the image of God, should shine unto them (2 Corinthians 4:4).

The location where Jesus was crucified was called "Golgotha." This word meant "place of the skull" in Hebrew. If we are to defeat satan, the first training field for spiritual warfare is in the mind—the place of the skull. The territory of the uncrucified thought life is the beachhead for satanic assault in our lives. To defeat the devil we must first be crucified in the place of the skull. The Holy Spirit renews us in the spirit of our mind. A growing believer will understand that the battlefield of the mind is the devil's playground.

But I Never Wanted to Be in a Battle

At my church, I preached a six-week series of sermons about the devil. I thought I did a tremendous job. I prayed and meditated about each message, did my research, and conducted a thorough exegesis of each Scripture passage. When it was over, I expected the congregation to have a complete understanding of satan's identity and work. I also expected them to have a more glorious appreciation of God.

For the most part, I accomplished my goal. Nevertheless, several well-meaning parishioners came to me and said, "Pastor, I don't want to have to fight the devil. I just want to remain a 'normal' Christian, go to church, mind my own business, and not cause trouble." They asked nicely, but they still urged me to tone the messages down a bit. A lot of devil-talk in the church can be very disquieting.

"Aren't we supposed to be learning about Jesus?" someone asked. "Aren't we supposed to learn about the good things concerning God?" asked another.

"Yes," I said, then I quickly added, "but it is imperative that, as followers of Christ, we talk, pray, and read about the person and personality of the enemy. We need to be aware of his devices as well as the power of God."

Knowledge is power. The power to defeat the enemy is readily available to us as people of God. Still, we are often ready prey for every subtle and overt attack. We become unwilling victims because of our own ignorance. We need to know who satan is and what he does. If we do not, satan rejoices over every downfall.

Since I completed that series of sermons, each one of those parishioners has come to me and thanked me for what he or she learned. They told me that they were attending to "business as usual" and trying to live a good Christian life; however, now when an attack comes to their doorstep, they recognize it as an attack of the enemy.

The enemy works in many ways today—some more subtle than others. Most Christians do not need to be persuaded that a war is on and a battle is raging. However, many do need to know how to fight the battle.

Ignorance Is a Fertile Field

Ignorance is a fertile field where satan plants error. Half-truths and unsound doctrine easily take root and grow. Knowledge and truth are slowly destroyed by the weeds of deception and confusion. God has created us to learn, absorb, and receive knowledge. Our minds do not want to remain empty. They crave information, regardless of its source. It is up to us to determine the kind of knowledge we will accept.

Satan and his servants can deceive us by appearing attractive, good, and moral. Many unsuspecting people follow smooth-talking, Bible-quoting leaders into cults that alienate them from their families and lead them into engaging in immorality, and practicing deceit. Do not be fooled by external appearances. Paul warns that satan can change himself into an angel of light. Even his servants can seem like godly ministers:

And no marvel; for Satan himself is transformed into an angel of light. Therefore it is no great thing if his ministers also be transformed as the ministers of righteousness; whose end shall be according to their works (2 Corinthians 11:14-15).

Our impressions alone are not accurate indicators of who is and who is not a true follower of Christ, so it helps to ask these questions:

1. Do their teachings confirm Scripture? (See Acts 17:11.)
2. Does the teacher affirm and proclaim that Jesus Christ is God, who came into this world as a man to save people from their sins? (See First John 4:1-3.)
3. Is the individual's lifestyle consistent with biblical morality? (See Matthew 12:33-37.)

Counterfeit Christianity

Satan inspires his *ministers* to imitate Christianity, and even do miracles (see Mt. 24:24; 2 Thess. 2:8-12; Rev. 13; 16:14; 19:20).

Where are satan's ministers, the ones who are transformed as ministers of righteousness? In Paul's day, the Corinthian believers fell for smooth talk—messages that sounded good and seemed to make sense. Today many false teachings still *seem* to make sense. Do not believe anyone simply because they sound like an authority or say things you like to hear.

Search the Bible and check people's words against God's Word. The Bible should be our authoritative guide for all teaching. During one of our youth meetings, several teens approached me and asked if I would arrange a special series of seminars to teach them about cults and New Age religions. There was a growing interest and curiosity among the young people in our community about this subject. In the last two years, a mosque, a Kingdom Hall, and a Christian Science reading room had sprung up near our church.

"The people seem nice," one teen said. "They always talk about Jesus." "The literature and tracts they pass out all say good things about Jesus and Christianity. Doesn't that make it ok?" another asked. These constant references to Jesus and Christianity raised questions and prompted interest throughout my congregation.

I seized this golden opportunity to explain to my entire congregation that satan and his evil spirits are very subtle. I taught them how he uses our ignorance as a device to draw mankind away from the true and living God.

"Many people in cults and New Age religions today," I explained, "are persons who at one time were part of a church family or were raised in a Christ-centered home." Their own ignorance of the Word of God and the subtle devices of satan led them astray. This falling away is usually accompanied by some great trauma or painful situation in a person's life. They then begin a frantic search for answers. False teachers can cloak themselves in business suits and bow ties and deliver good sermons. They can quote Scripture, sing hymns, and call Jesus by name.

If one neglects to study the Word, one may fall prey to satan's devices through simple ignorance. Ignorance is one of the chief means used by satan and his forces to control individuals. Our own ignorance of God's Word accounts for satan's widespread success in getting men to accept his suggestions, doctrines, ideas, leadings, and guidance. False teachers distort the truth about Christ and end up preaching *a different Christ, a different Spirit,* and *a different salvation.* Because the Bible is God's infallible Word, those who teach anything different are both mistaken and misleading their followers. As believers, we are individually responsible for knowing God's truth.

> *For if he that cometh preacheth another Jesus, whom we have not preached, or if ye receive another spirit, which ye have not received, or another gospel, which ye have not accepted, ye might well bear with him* (2 Corinthians 11:4).

> *Study to shew thyself approved unto God...rightly dividing the word of truth* (2 Timothy 2:15).

> *...Thy truth* [shall] *continually preserve me* (Psalm 40:11).

> *Jesus saith unto him, I am the way, the truth, and the life...* (John 14:6).

> *Howbeit when He, the Spirit of truth, is come, He will guide you into all truth...* (John 16:13).

> *We are of God: he that knoweth God heareth us; he that is not of God heareth not us. Hereby know we the spirit of truth...* (1 John 4:6).

Detecting Good and Evil Spirits

Scripture outlines definite ways to detect what kind of spirit is seeking to control an individual. These guiding principles are useful for detecting both good and evil spirits, as well as their operations and doctrine:

1. Any doctrine that denies anything taught in Scripture or causes doubt and unbelief concerning it is from satan and his demons (see 1 Tim. 4:1-8). Any religion denying the inspiration of the Bible; the reality of God as a person; the virgin birth

and divinity of Christ; His miraculous power and supernatural ministry; the death, burial, bodily resurrection, and bodily manifestation of Christ after His resurrection; the bodily ascension of Jesus to Heaven and His return to set up an eternal Kingdom in the world; the necessity of the new birth, cleansing from sin, and living free from it; or the numerous other experiences of the Bible is yielding to "the spirit of error" and not "the spirit of truth" (1 Jn. 4:1-6). These fundamental truths cannot be denied. (See John 8:47; Romans 1:16; Philippians 2:11; Second Timothy 3:16.)

2. Any power, influence, or doctrine that causes one to become passive, inactive, and submissive (failing to resist supernatural spirits seeking to control one's life in ways contrary to the teachings of Scripture) is not of God. The Bible says "Resist the devil..." (Jas. 4:7b; see also 1 Pet. 5:8-9). Any inclination to approve sin, ignore the necessity of repentance and holy living, promote a tendency to remove the penalty for sin, and cast doubt that hell is literal and eternal is promoted by satan, not God. Just as God requires truth in order for the Holy Spirit to work in a life, the devil requires men to believe lies. When they do, he holds them in bondage (see 1 Cor. 6:9-11; Gal. 5:19-21; 6:7-8; Eph. 6:10-18; 1 Tim. 4:1-9).

3. The Holy Spirit can be recognized by the fruit of the Spirit mentioned in Galatians 5:22-23 (love, joy, peace, longsuffering, gentleness, goodness, faith, meekness, and temperance).

Knowing God's divine will is an earmark of Holy Spirit manifestation. Always remember that First John 4:1a commands, "...try the spirits whether they are of God."

A Spiritual Dynamo

Most of us have seen advertisements showing a 98-pound weakling getting sand kicked in his face by a huge beach bully.

The muscle-bound loudmouth then walks off with the poor guy's girlfriend. The next scene shows the discouraged young man starting a muscle-building program. He vows fervently that he will never be humiliated like that again. We are then shown that after a few short months of intensive exercise, he develops into an exemplary specimen of manhood. The last frame shows our hero delivering a well-aimed blow to the jaw of the bully with the appropriate caption, "Take that you rat, and don't ever bother my girl again."

On a spiritual level, God wants to turn you into a spiritual dynamo so that you can stand up to satan, the bully of the universe, and tell him that he cannot take advantage of you. Jesus tells us how we are to live now that He has defeated the enemy. He says:

And these signs shall follow them that believe; In My name they shall cast out devils; they shall speak with new tongues; they shall take up serpents; and if they drink any deadly thing, it shall not hurt them; they shall lay hands on the sick, and they shall recover (Mark 16:17-18).

If you find that your shield of protection has holes in it and your breastplate of righteousness has fallen down around your knees, take heart. There is hope for you. *You too can be an overcomer in the name of Jesus.* This does not mean that you will be looking for demons to attack. It simply means that you will not have to put up with being knocked around or confused by their disruptive activities. You will be able to stop them in their tracks when they pop up their heads. As a result, you will live a victorious Christian life. We are told in Second Timothy 1:7 that God has not given us the spirit of fear but one of power, love, and a sound mind. Is this what you want? Let me show you how you can be more than a conqueror through Him that loved you. (See Romans 8:37.)

The Mind in Rebellion

Paul says that the carnal or sinful mind is against God. Such a mind will not obey the law of God, nor can it because it submits to sin. When the mind ceases to rebel, then it ceases to sin. As long as the mind and will of an individual lives in rebellion, it cannot please God "because the carnal mind is enmity against God: for it is not subject to the law of God, neither indeed can be" (Rom. 8:7).

We must always remember that, as believers, we are redeemed people living in a fallen world. Therefore we must live our faith every day. When sacrificing an animal according to God's law, the Old Testament priest killed the animal, cut it in pieces, and placed it on the altar. Sacrifice was important, but even in the Old Testament God made it clear that obedience from the heart was much more important.

...Hath the Lord as great delight in burnt offerings and sacrifices, as in obeying the voice of the Lord? Behold, to obey is better than sacrifice, and to hearken than the fat of rams (1 Samuel 15:22).

God wants us to offer ourselves, not animals, as living sacrifices—daily laying aside our own desires to follow Him (see Rom. 12:1). God wants us to put all our energy and resources at His disposal and trust Him to guide us. We do this out of gratitude because our sins have been forgiven. God has good, acceptable, and perfect plans for His children (see Rom. 12:2). He wants us to be *new* people with *renewed* minds, living to honor and obey Him. He wants only what is best for us. He gave His Son to make our new lives possible. Therefore, we should joyfully volunteer as living sacrifices for His service.

Renewing the Mind

Believers are called to "not be conformed to this world" with its behavior and customs that are usually selfish and often corrupt (Rom. 12:2). Many Christians wisely decide that worldly behavior is off-limits for them. Our refusal to conform to this world's values, however, must go even deeper than the level of our behavior and customs. It must be firmly founded in our minds. It is possible to avoid most worldly customs and still be proud, covetous, selfish, stubborn, and arrogant.

Only when the Holy Spirit renews, reeducates, and redirects our mind will we be truly transformed. Paul divided people into two categories—those who allow themselves to be controlled by their sinful nature, and those who follow after the Holy Spirit (see Rom. 8:1-17). We would all be in the first category if Jesus had not offered us a way out. Once we say "Yes" to Jesus, we will want to continue following Him because His way brings life and peace.

We must consciously choose to center our mind on God daily by using the Bible to discover God's guidelines and follow them. We should ask ourselves, "What does Jesus want me to do?" in every perplexing situation. When the Holy Spirit points out the right way, do it eagerly.

For they that are after the flesh do mind the things of the flesh; but they that are after the Spirit the things of the Spirit (Romans 8:5).

Paul goes on to say that "...to be carnally minded is death; but to be spiritually minded is life and peace" (Rom. 8:6). The human mind that dwells on worldly things is at enmity with God because it is not subject to the law of God. As a pastor, I can predict the growth potential of every new convert who receives Christ and comes into our church by his or her level of interest and attendance to Bible study. The renewal of the mind is crucial to the growth and success of spiritual maturity.

A New Mindset

Sometimes we have the same mindset, or pattern of thinking, that Israel had in the wilderness. Although they were free, they still thought like slaves. They had been oppressed for 400 years. They could not believe good things because of all the bad things that had happened to them in the past. God delivered them from the Egyptians, yet they still limited God with their slave mentality. Their hands and feet were free, but their minds remained in shackles.

Past problems and failures can condition you to give up and limit God. When I was in college studying to become a teacher, we studied the experiments of Pavlov, a noted behavioral psychologist. Through various experiments, he found that an animal could be conditioned to give up by repeated failure.

In one experiment, Pavlov presented a biscuit to a dog. The animal was then tied to a leash that was too short for it to reach the treat. The dog leaped for the treat for hours. However, after repeated attempts to get the treat failed, the animal lost all desire to even try and so gave up. He had been conditioned to expect failure.

Satan reminds us of our past failures and indiscretions so we will remain hindered in our spiritual growth. Unlike Pavlov's animals, we have a choice. We can either fight the conditioning that repeated failure tries to impose on us or give in and give up. God not only cares, He has provided a cure. God's Word says, "For though a righteous man falls seven times, he rises again..." (Prov. 24:16 NIV).

The Cure

Chronic illness, addiction, marital problems, desperate financial problems: everyone has barriers in their lives, things that hold them back and keep them from being all they want to be in Christ. Barriers are those tough, deeply rooted things in your life that refuse to change or those things that you have just given up on. Perhaps you have tried and tried to break free without success. Maybe you have fasted, prayed, had counseling, submitted to prayer for deliverance, and have done everything you know how to do. Do not be discouraged. You can overcome and can find victory through the renewal of your mind from God's Word. In order to renew the mind one must:

1. Read
2. Apply
3. Wait

Read

The Word of God contains hidden treasures of knowledge. Every human situation we encounter in this life has a parallel situation in Scripture. The customs and minor details may be different, but the overall underlying circumstances of the human drama have already been played out on those ancient stages.

The Bible is a book of divine wisdom. *Knowledge* is "the state or fact of knowing gained through experience or study." *Wisdom* is "the understanding of what is true, right, or lasting." We must seek after divine knowledge and wisdom by reading and studying God's Word. The athlete who uses his mind has an advantage over a physically stronger but unthinking opponent. *The thinking athlete assesses the situation and plans strategies*. Wisdom, not muscle, has put humankind in charge of the animal kingdom. We exercise regularly and eat well to build our physical strength. We must also take equal pains to develop wisdom because wisdom from God's Word is a vital part of spiritual strength.

In this age of information, knowledge is plentiful but wisdom is scarce. Wisdom means far more than simply *knowing* information. It is a basic attitude that affects every aspect of life. Wisdom is the revealed mind of God. By reading about Jesus' earthly ministry, we can see wisdom in action.

Apply

I am so grateful for the many hours I spent as a child in Sunday school studying God's Word. Those years of study gave me a firm foundation of wisdom and knowledge that I have drawn upon time after time when I've encountered adversity in my life.

As a teenager, I often heard older people in the church talk about "taking authority" over the enemy satan. I was told, "The name of Jesus is in and of itself a weapon against the devil." I was also taught that "as believers, we can speak to the devil in Jesus' name and control his influence over our life."

How could I dare "speak to" the devil? The very thought seemed ludicrous. Many believers would never dare to speak directly to satan, even in the name of Jesus. They have been tyrannized and traumatized by the prevailing theology of his power and invincibility.

Then I remembered the story in Luke 4 of how Jesus confronted satan in the wilderness, and the account of how He rebuked satan as he worked through Peter in Matthew 16. I realized that Jesus never felt reticent about speaking to the evil powers of darkness, so why should I?

In order to keep one's mind renewed, one must not only read, but also apply the principles and strategies of God's Word. For years I could not imagine satan running away from *me*. The picture that terrified me the most was the one of satan on the attack "seeking whom he may devour" (1 Pet. 5:8). However, James' exhortation to resist him encouraged me to face the devil head on as I followed Jesus' example (see Jas. 4:7). When I applied the Word of God and mustered enough courage to speak directly to satan in the name of Jesus, I was surprised and delighted to discover an immediate sense of deliverance. Satan fled in fear at the mere mention of Jesus' name.

By itself, our resistance is not what causes satan to flee. The devil flees because of the power of God that we apply when he attacks us. As he sang God's praises for enabling his people to triumph over their enemies, the psalmist said, "Through Thee will we push down our enemies: through Thy name we will tread them under that rise up against us" (Ps. 44:5).

Jesus' disciples saw tremendous results as they ministered in Jesus' name and with His authority. They applied the principles and teachings they learned from Jesus to every attack of satan. The victories they witnessed elated them—"And the seventy returned again with joy, saying, Lord, even the devils are subject unto us through Thy name" (Lk. 10:17).

God promises to give us, as believers, power over every work of evil when we apply the principles of His Word.

Wait

After we have read, studied, and applied God's Word to our lives, then comes the most difficult part—waiting. We need to take a certain posture while waiting for God to work on our behalf. We should wait prayerfully, patiently, expectantly, single-mindedly, and continually. If we wait with the proper mindset, God will use that *waiting time* to renew our strength, courage, and trust in Him. David waited on God all day. He was a man after God's own heart, and he knew the secret of waiting on God: "Lead me in Thy truth, and teach me: for Thou art the God of my salvation; on Thee do I wait all the day" (Ps. 25:5).

Isaiah decided to wait for God's help even though many of his prophecies would not come true for 700 years (some of them are still awaiting fulfillment). Isaiah proclaimed, "And I will wait upon the Lord...and I will look for Him" (Is. 8:17).

Waiting on God is synonymous with trusting Him. In order to wait properly, one must have faith, confidence, trust, and hope in whatever promises have been spoken by Him in His Word. Micah showed great faith in God as he proclaimed that he would wait upon God because God hears and saves when help is needed. "Therefore I will look unto the Lord; I will wait for the God of my salvation: my God will hear me" (Mic. 7:7).

We too can have a relationship with God that will allow us to have confidence like Micah. It does not take unusual talent. It simply takes faith in God and a willingness to act on that faith.

God Watches and Directs

We are often confused by the events around us. Many things happen that we will never understand in this life. Other things will fall into place in the future as we look back over the years and see how God worked. Most important, God's Word counsels us not to worry if we do not understand everything as it happens (see Mt. 6:25-34).

Satan uses worry and fear to torment us in his playground of the human mind. We should trust that God knows what He is doing, even if His timing or design is not clear to us. God watches over and directs every step that we take. "The steps of a good man are ordered by the Lord: and He delighteth in his way" (Ps. 37:23).

David knew from experience what it meant to wait on the Lord. He had been anointed king at the age of 16, but he did not become king until he was 30. During the interim, he was chased through the wilderness by jealous King Saul. David had to wait on God for the fulfillment of his promise to reign. Later, after becoming king, he was chased by his rebellious son, Absalom. (See 2 Samuel 1-2, 15.)

Waiting on God is not easy! It often seems He is not answering our prayers or does not understand the urgency of our situation. This kind of thinking implies that God is not in control or is not fair. However, God is not a God who is moved by crisis. He does not respond to our urgency to get out of our tight spots. Even though it may look like chaos, God has a plan for each of our lives. God uses our waiting times to refresh, renew, and teach us. Finally, even the strongest people become tired at times, yet God's power and strength never diminishes. His strength is our source of strength.

> *But they that wait upon the Lord shall renew their strength; they shall mount up with wings as eagles; they shall run, and not be weary; and they shall walk, and not faint* (Isaiah 40:31).

When you feel as if life is crushing you and you cannot go another step, remember that you can call upon God to renew your strength. Pray this renewal prayer:

> *Lord, renew my mind, heal my thinking, and touch my spirit. Help me to defeat satan on the battleground of my mind. Guard my thoughts. As I study Your Word, help me to read, apply, and wait. Give me the mind of Christ so that I may think and move according to the leading and guiding of the Holy Spirit in my life. Amen.*

Chapter 3

SATAN'S JOB DESCRIPTION

*Be sober, be vigilant; because your adversary
the devil, as a roaring lion, walketh about,
seeking whom he may devour.*
1 Peter 5:8

WHO IS satan and what does he want from us? Satan is our archenemy. Scripture clearly confirms that he is the foe of every human being, beginning with Adam and Eve (see Jas. 4:4). The name *satan* actually means "adversary, or one who opposes." Yet any discussion about warfare with this enemy tends to repel many believers. Some Christians become upset when time is spent talking about the devil. However, one way to know God is to recognize who satan is. Satan works best in places of darkness, ignorance, and blindness, where there is a lack of understanding.

What and who is satan? And what does he want from me? Satan is not an evil principal or abstract power. He is not a disease

---

germ or an error of the mortal mind; nor is he a being with hoofs, horns, and a tail. He is not dressed in a red suit, and he does not hold a pitchfork. To the contrary, satan is a person with a specific personality, distinctive traits, and characteristics. He has personal names and a personal plan to oppose the will of God throughout the earth.

Satan's Personal Names and Titles

This is a list of scriptural references to satan:

1. lucifer (Is. 14:12-14)
2. devil and satan (Rev. 12:9)
3. beelzebub (Mt. 10:25; 12:24)
4. belial (2 Cor. 6:15)
5. adversary (1 Pet. 5:8-9)
6. dragon (Rev. 12:3-12; 13:1-4; 20:1-3)
7. serpent (2 Cor. 11:3; Rev. 12:9)
8. god of this world (2 Cor. 4:4)
9. prince of this world (Jn. 12:31)
10. prince of the power of the air (Eph. 2:1-3)
11. accuser of the brethren (Rev. 12:10)
12. enemy (Mt. 4:3)
13. tempter (Mt. 4:1-10)
14. (the) wicked one (Mt. 13:19,38)
15. (that) wicked one (1 Jn. 5:18)

Historically speaking, satan is not mentioned by name until we see him in the Book of Job.

Now there was a day when the sons of God came to present themselves before the Lord, and Satan came also among them (Job 1:6).

He is not even mentioned by name in the Book of Genesis. It is clear, however, in Genesis chapter 3, that satan is the subtle enemy of humankind. He used the serpent as a tool to cause Adam and Eve to transgress God's Word.

*Now the serpent was more subtil than any beast of
the field which the Lord God had made. And he said
unto the woman, Yea, hath God said, Ye shall not eat
of every tree of the garden?* (Genesis 3:1)

In First Peter 5:8 satan does not appear as himself, but he is
likened unto a roaring lion. In Matthew 16 he is the unseen enemy when Jesus tells His disciples about His imminent death
and resurrection. Satan uses the disciple Peter to rebuke Jesus
for His sayings.

*But He turned, and said unto Peter, Get thee behind
Me, Satan: thou art an offence unto Me: for thou sa-
vorest not the things that be of God, but those that be
of men* (Matthew 16:23).

Who is satan? Job 1–2 says that when the angels came to
present themselves before the Lord, satan came also. Therefore, we know that he has access to Heaven. He associates
with angels. He carries on conversations with God. He is the
propagator of sickness and disease in the body. He is the accuser of the brethren. He hates good people, and he recog-
nizes and envies the blessings of God upon others.

Satan works best when we are ignorant of who he is and
what he does. He operates more effectively in darkness. A better understanding of evil, darkness, and satan gives us a clearer
understanding of good, light, and God.

The Origin of Satan

God created satan with other beings, principalities, and
powers in Heaven and earth (see Job 38:4-7; Ezek. 28:11-17;
Col. 1:15-18). According to Isaiah 14:12-14, Jeremiah 4:23-26,
Ezekiel 28:11-17, and other passages, satan, known as lucifer,
had a kingdom on earth long before the six days of creation
and Adam accounted in Genesis 1:3-2:25. These passages

reveal that he fell, led an invasion into Heaven, and was defeated. At that time the earth was cursed and all life was destroyed by the first flood (see Gen. 1:2).

Satan regained rulership over the earth in Adam's day by causing mankind's fall and usurping his dominion. His relations to mankind throughout the ages has continued to be that of a usurper. As long as man tolerates Satan's dictatorship, he will remain subject to him. Now each individual can, by the power of the gospel, defeat satan and rid himself of all demonic relationships. This is what God demands, and He has provided the means for it to happen.

> *Behold, I give unto you power to tread on serpents and scorpions, and over all the power of the enemy: and nothing shall by any means hurt you* (Luke 10:19).

Satan's present position as ruler of this world's system and as the prince of this world will be ended forever when Christ comes. Man will again inherit the earth and live in it forever.

> *And the devil that deceived them was cast into the lake of fire and brimstone, where the beast and the false prophet are, and shall be tormented day and night for ever and ever* (Revelation 20:10).

> *And God shall wipe away all tears from their eyes; and there shall be no more death, neither sorrow, nor crying, neither shall there be any more pain: for the former things are passed away* (Revelation 21:4).

Demons in History

What are demons? Demons are fallen angels who joined satan in his rebellion against God. They are now evil spirits under satan's control. They help satan tempt people to sin and have great destructive powers.

Both the Old Testament and the New Testament Epistles are almost silent on the subject. The Hebrew word for demon (*sed*) is borrowed from the Babylonians. In Babylon, demons were thought to be supernatural powers, neither good nor evil. The Babylonians believed that demons exercised power over humans at their own will and whim. The Greeks thought demons were supernatural powers that inhabited the air close to earth, someplace between men and the gods. The Greeks believed demons had an evil influence on human affairs, caused misery and disaster, were agents of madness and distress, and caused many of their sicknesses. The Greeks viewed demons as hostile beings that must be appeased or controlled by magic.

Later Judaism showed considerable interest in demons. Demons were thought of as malignant beings distinct from angels, and a number of theories were suggested to explain their existence. One theory held that demons were the offspring of a primeval mating of fallen angels with human women (see Gen. 6:1-4). The rabbis believed the demons were eager to lead humanity into sin. They also believed that they were the cause of much, but not every sickness.

Demons in Old Testament Scripture

In view of the common beliefs held by most ancient cultures, it is striking to find only two specific references to demons in the Old Testament. These passages refer to the rebellious generation that died in the wilderness.

They sacrificed unto devils, not to God; to gods whom they knew not, to new gods that came newly up, whom your fathers feared not (Deuteronomy 32:17).

And they served their idols: which were a snare unto them. Yea, they sacrificed their sons and their daughters unto devils (Psalm 106:36-37).

Both of these passages suggest that real demonic beings existed behind the gods and goddesses of the pagans. This is something Paul affirms in First Corinthians: that the sacrifices of pagans were offered to demons (see 1 Cor. 10:20).

The Old Testament contains prohibitions against all spiritism and magic, both of which were linked with the demonic in every ancient culture. There are other hints in such passages as First Samuel 28:13 and Isaiah 8:19. Still, very little attention is paid to demons in the Old Testament. Instead, the Old Testament concentrates on God, the Creator and Redeemer, who is sovereign over every power—natural and supernatural.

Demons in New Testament Scripture

Although the Old Testament is relatively silent about demons, the Gospels are full of references to demonic activity. Jesus, during His ministry of healing and restoration of the oppressed, exposed many demons. One reason may be that satan's kingdom concentrated unusual forces on Palestine while Jesus walked that land. Gospel references to demons show them possessing or oppressing human beings. Demonic influence was expressed in various sicknesses and in madness. When some observers argued that Jesus was mad or in league with satan, "Others said...Can a devil open the eyes of the blind?" (Jn. 10:21)

The Gospels show Jesus driving out demons wherever He met them. Confronted by Jesus, demonic forces lost their power. Jesus' own defense against the charge is based on this: How could satan's kingdom stand if he drove out his own demonic power? Any divided kingdom must soon fall (see Lk. 11:14-22).

The Gospels do picture demons as living beings with malignant powers. Demons are personal beings, not impersonal influences. Jesus demonstrated His total mastery of demons, expelling them with a word. However fearsome demons may be, the person who walks with God has nothing to fear. After Jesus returned to Heaven, little demonic activity is reported by the Bible. Acts 5, 8, and 19 mention evil spirits. The Epistles do not. Romans 8:38 establishes the dichotomy between angels and demons. In First Corinthians 10:20-21, Paul warns that demonic beings are the spiritual realities behind the facades of idolatry. In First Timothy 4:1, he suggests that demons distort truth and encourage the spread of twisted doctrines of their own. Aside from brief views of increased demonic activity at history's end (Book of Revelation), this is all that the New Testament has to say about demons.

Particular note should be taken of the Epistles' comparative silence on the demonic. Although there are many passages that deal with Christian life and ministry, none speak of demons. There are no guidelines for exorcism. There are no warnings against demon possession. There is no hint of terror or awe, no suggestion that we should fear or pay special attention to these unseen evil powers.

What Do Demons Do?

Demonic spirits work to tempt people to sin. There are evil spiritual beings who can and do influence events on the earth. We learn from the Gospels that they can possess and oppress human beings. They can bring misery and cause sickness. Demons were not created by satan because God is the Creator of all; rather, they are fallen angels who joined satan in his rebellion. In their degenerate state they cause great tragedy and crises in the lives of individuals.

However, in every case where demons encountered Jesus, they lost their power. God limits what they can do. There is no doubt that Jesus has total power over demons. He exercised that power in New Testament times and cast them out. Jesus did not rely on any rite or magical words. He simply commanded and the demons obeyed. Demons recognized Jesus as God's Son, but they did not think they had to obey Him (see Mt. 8:29). Later, when the disciples cast out demons, they commanded the demons in Jesus' name, but the name was not enough. A personal relationship with Jesus was also essential (see Acts 16:16-18; 19:13-16).

You may believe Jesus is the Son of God, but *just believing* is not enough. Faith is more than belief. By faith we must accept what God has done for us by saving us from sin. Then we must live out our faith by developing an intimate relationship with God and obeying His Word.

Possession and Oppression

A believer cannot be *possessed* by satan or his demons. It is hard to imagine a demon or satan himself, settling comfortably into any association with a person indwelt by the very Spirit of God. However, a believer can be *oppressed*, *suppressed*, and *harassed* by satanic and demonic activity. We still live in a fallen world; therefore, we must expect that satan will attack us from time to time. On the other hand, a non-believer can be *possessed* or totally influenced by satan and his evil spirits.

Many psychologists dismiss accounts of demon possession as a primitive way to describe mental illness. Clearly, however, a demon controlled the man described in Mark 1. The Book of Mark emphasizes Jesus' conflict with evil powers to show his superiority over them, and it records many stories about Jesus casting out demons. Jesus did not have to conduct an elaborate exorcism ritual. His Word was enough to send out the demons. "And He...cast out many devils; and suffered not the devils to speak, because they knew Him" (Mk. 1:34).

Occult Fascination

Even today, demons are dangerous, powerful, and destructive. While it is important to recognize their evil activity so that we can stay away from them, we must avoid any curiosity about or involvement with demonic forces or the occult. Just as most of us are naturally curious about magic tricks, the Israelites were curious about the occult practices of the Canaanite religions. Satan is behind the occult.

Today people are still fascinated by horoscopes, fortune-telling, witchcraft, and bizarre cults. Their interest often comes from a desire to know and control the future. However, satan is no less dangerous today than he was in Moses' time. In the Bible, God tells us all we need to know about what is going to happen. The information satan offers is likely to either be distorted or completely false.

With the trustworthy guidance of the Holy Spirit through the Scriptures and the Church, we do not need to turn to occult sources for faulty information about our future. God warned His people in Deuteronomy not to practice black magic, or call on demon spirits for aid, or be a fortune teller, a serpent charmer, a medium, a wizard, a witch, or call forth the spirits of the dead. Anyone doing these things was, and still is, an object of horror and disgust to the Lord.

For all that do these things are an abomination unto the Lord: and because of these abominations the Lord thy God doth drive them out from before thee (Deuteronomy 18:12).

The battle with satan is a difficult on-going struggle. Victory over sin and temptation comes through faith in Jesus Christ, not through our own efforts. The good news is that if we resist satan and his demonic influences, he will flee from us (see Jas. 4:7).

A Personal Experience

I remember my first known experience with demonic activity. I was in college, attending a rather innocent-looking social gathering of freshmen girls. It was Friday night, and we were having a pajama party in the girl's dorm. The popcorn and soda had run out and everyone was getting bored. A few girls drifted back to their room, but I hung around to see what might happen next. Just then one of the girls piped up and said, "*Hey, let's play Ouija Board.*" Well, I did not know what a Ouija board was, but I was game. Everyone else seemed excited so I thought I should be too.

The girl in charge returned from her dorm room with a large mysterious box under her arm. *Scrabble or Bingo*, I thought, *it will be harmless*. She quieted everyone in the room and turned the lights down low for *atmosphere* as she explained the Ouija board. I watched with great curiosity as each player gently placed her fingers on the board. *Big deal*, I thought, waiting patiently in line for my turn.

Finally, I stepped up to the table holding the board and took my seat. My questions were easy. I wanted to know what most naive 18-year-old girls want to know. "*Who will I marry? How many children will I have? Will I have a date for the homecoming dance?*" Heavy stuff!

Just then we were startled by the sound of a blood-curdling scream that pierced the silence of the gloomy dark room. I turned to see a girl running frantically down the hallway in her underwear. I bolted from the room in fear, and everyone else scattered out of sheer terror. It seems that the Ouija board "told" her that she was possessed with demons and that the devil would be coming to get her that night. The girl could not be consoled. Pandemonium broke out. An unexplained fear gripped all of us. Someone pulled the fire alarm. The dorm mother awakened. Campus security was summoned and the township police arrived. What a mess, all from a seemingly senseless juvenile game. The girl was rushed to the hospital. We later learned that she suffered such severe emotional trauma that she was not able to return to college that year. Needless to say, our entire dorm was placed on campus restriction for the rest of that semester. All of this devil and demon talk was foreign to me, but that was the beginning and ending of my curiosity and interest in anything associated with the occult.

Demons seem to hold a strong fascination for some of us. Yes, demons are real! Just as satan is free to trouble humanity, so are the fallen angels. What a joy it is to know that their fate is defined in Scripture: "...Depart from Me, ye cursed, into everlasting fire, prepared for the devil and his angels" (Mt. 25:41).

Greater Is He

The devil is subject to us. *We* tell *him* what to do. He cannot exercise control over us without our permission. God has given us power, as believers, over every work of satan.

Behold, I give unto you power to tread on serpents and scorpions, and over all the power of the enemy: and nothing shall be any means hurt you (Lk. 10:19).

What an awesome revelation! This means that satan cannot do anything to destroy me. I have reached the point in my life that when I do encounter problems, I am able to view them as *minor difficulties, setbacks,* and *temporary inconveniences* because I always expect God to cause all things to "work together for my good" (see Rom. 8:28). I immediately remind myself that:

1. I belong to God.
2. I have already won every fight with those who are against God.
3. The Holy Spirit in my heart is stronger than any evil in this wicked world.

Ye are of God, little children, and have overcome them: because greater is He [Holy Spirit] *that is in you, than he that is in the world* (1 John 4:4).

It is easy to be frightened by the wickedness we see all around us. Evil is obviously much stronger than we are. John assures us, however, that God is stronger yet. When satan seems to be getting the upper hand in your life, it is because you are not taking advantage of the power of God that is readily available to you. You are like a *millionaire* living in poverty because you are not aware of the riches available to you.

Satan's Eternal Career

The devil has a career. A career is a chosen pursuit, a life work, a specialty, or a profession. Satan has an eternal career. His chosen pursuit and life work will not change. Satan has a full-time job attempting to destroy the relationship and fellowship that God wants to have with you. He never sleeps! It is almost as if satan *gets up early in the morning and stays up late at night* devising a wicked plan to get you to believe that Bible study is unimportant, prayer is ineffective, church attendance is unnecessary, righteous living is impossible, tithing is unbiblical, and commitment to God is unreasonable.

When his plans and assignments are carried out and completed, guess what the devil does? He has a party. He celebrates and rejoices over the faults and the failures of the saints. Demons hang the crepe paper and set out the mints and trail mix. They turn the lights down low and bring out the noise makers, and the devil blows up balloons. Then he goes over to the stereo and dusts off some of his best hits; his oldies but goodies like "Heatwave" and "Great Balls of Fire."

What is the devil doing? He is having a party, celebrating your downfall, and rejoicing over your defeat. Can't you see him and all of his demons rejoicing over your every downfall? What a party! The devil is blowing up balloons at the party he is throwing in hell for you. His guest list is extensive. An open invitation is extended to all of those who refuse to trust God and apply His Word to their lives.

Satan *celebrates* every time he succeeds in chasing you out of the church or damaging your enthusiasm so that your attendance is sporadic. Hell becomes happy when you settle for compromises instead of striving to live holy. Demons are ecstatic over every day-to-day failure when you fail to apply the principles of God's Word to your life. Demonic forces are always on the lookout for new recruits.

War on the Saints

In the Old Testament, satan's great work caused the fall of man, usurped his dominion, and attempted to prevent the coming of the Messiah into the world. He did this in order to avert his own defeat and pending doom.

Today satan is busy counterfeiting the scriptural doctrines and experiences of God. He considers this work a very important part of his plan to deceive the saints. As believers, we are commanded to prove and test all doctrines and experiences in the supernatural realm to see if they are of God or of satan (see 1 Thess. 5:21; Rom. 12:2). It is certain that every religion, doctrine, and experience among mankind cannot be of God.

The knowledge of truth is the first essential in warfare against demons and error. Believers are in great danger when they accept anything and everything in the realm of the supernatural as *from the Lord*. The fact that a believer is a child of God does not stop the devil from trying, in every conceivable way, to imitate God. Believers are the ones that satan concentrates on and wars against.

Satan Searches

Satan searches for uncommitted, wishy-washy believers. He seeks out those who have no real stability in God and can be easily influenced by evil. He prowls around on Bible study night, making a list of those who (for no valid reason) never attend. He keeps a record of church members who only attend on holidays. He maintains a very extensive rolodex for those he can always count on to cause strife and fuel gossip in the church. Satan's address book is always filled with the names of believers who are his potential party-goers. Satan still exercises great power in the world. He is called the "prince of the air," and he is at work in all who are disobedient to God.

Holy Attributes

As children of God, we must understand that our heavenly Father is good. His chief motivation for our lives is to make us like Christ. Everything God does, as He deals with us in our Christian life, is to develop our potential to the greatest degree possible. On the other hand, satan is totally evil. Jesus gives us satan's job description in John 10:10 when He says that all he (satan) does is to steal, kill, and destroy. To better understand who God is, we need to look at the attributes or the characteristics of God that He has revealed about Himself:

1. He is a spirit being with a personal spirit body, soul, and spirit through which He manifests Himself (see 1 Jn. 3:24).
2. He is invisible (see Col. 1:15).
3. He is immortal (see 1 Tim. 1:17).
4. He is eternal (see 1 Tim. 1:17).
5. He is infinite in presence (see 1 Kings 8:27).
6. He is infinite in power (see Mt. 28:18).
7. He is infinite in His acts (see Mt. 19:26).

8. He is infinite in time and knowledge (see Deut. 33:27; Ps. 90:2; Is. 57:15; Rom. 11:33).
9. He is infinite in greatness (see Ps. 145:3).
10. He is omnipotent (all powerful) (see Rev. 19:6).

He can do all things consistent with His nature and plan, but He cannot lie or act contrary to Himself.

11. He is omnipresent (not omnibody) (see 1 Kings 8:27; Ps. 139:7-12).

His presence is not governed by bodily contact, but by knowledge and relationship. God's body is not omnipresent, for it is only at one place at one time, like others, but His presence can be *realized* any place where persons know Him and seek Him.

12. He is omniscient (all-knowing) as far as His nature, plan, and work are concerned (see Acts 1:24;15:18). God knows certain things about free moral agents. See Genesis 6:5-7; 11:5-7; 18:21; 22:12; Second Chronicles 16:9; Job 12:22; 24:23; Psalm 7:9; 44:21; 139:1-6; Proverbs 24:12; Jeremiah 17:10; and Ezekiel 11:5.

God sends messengers on innumerable duties to help Him carry out His rulership of all things. See Daniel 10:13-21; 11:1; 12:1; Zechariah 1:7-11; 6:1-8; Matthew 18:10-11; and Hebrews 1:14. God permits free moral agents freedom of action regarding their conduct and destiny (see Rom. 8:29).

13. He is life (see Jer. 10:10; Jn. 5:26; 1 Thess. 1:9; Heb. 7:16; Rev. 11:11).
14. He is self-existent (see Ex. 3:4; Jn. 1:4; 5:26).
15. He is immutable (see Ps. 102:27; Mal. 3:6; 2 Tim. 2:13; Heb. 6:18; Jas. 1:17).

God is immutable regarding His plan for the highest good of human beings and of the universe. His plan includes the change of methods or ways to save as many people as possible. For example, when He abolished the Law of Moses, it was not an unexpected change in God's plan, but rather the execution of that plan. When humankind fell and God had to send Christ, it was simply the fulfillment of the plan. The plan was made to be executed when obedience was rendered and terms met. When the terms are not met, it is not failure or change with God, but with man.

16. He is perfect (see Deut. 32:4; Ps. 18:30; Mt. 5:48).

If any imperfection is noted in creation or redemption, it is sin and rebellion in the free moral agents that have caused it. God does not change His original plan of creation and redemption. He plans to redeem and restore all creation, except those who rebel against Him, to original perfection. (See Acts 3:21; Ephesians 1:10; and Revelation 21-22.)

17. He is the truth and the perfect harmony of God's Word (see Deut. 32:4; Jn. 17:3; 1 Jn. 5:20).
18. He is wisdom (see Rom. 11:33; 1 Tim. 1:17).
19. He is love and His infinite goodness communicates His love to others (see Jn. 3:16; Rom. 15:30; 1 Jn. 4:8).
20. He is holy and absolutely pure in nature (see Ex. 15:11; Is. 6:3; 1 Pet. 1:16).
21. He is righteous and all His acts are right (see Rom. 3:21-26; Heb. 12:5-12; 1 Jn. 1:9).
22. He is faithful and absolutely trustworthy (see 1 Cor. 10:13; 2 Cor. 1:20; Heb. 6:18).
23. He is merciful. His divine mercy manifests to relieve His creation of suffering (see Rom. 12:1-2; 2 Cor. 1:3; Tit. 3:5).
24. He is good. His divine goodness preserves life and extends mercy (see Mt. 5:45; Rom. 2:4; Acts 14:17).
25. He is provident in that He cares and provides for all His creation (see Job 38:41; Ps. 30:6).

All these attributes require a conception of God as having a soul of feelings, emotions, passions, desires, a spirit of intelligence, will, choice, powers, self-consciousness, self-determination, and a spirit body through which these faculties are manifest.

God never acts out of character. His attributes never get out of balance with each other. For this reason, we are able to trust Him and have confidence in His judgment concerning our lives. God will always do what is best for us. He is totally wise, good, and just. His love for us is beyond understanding. Why should anyone ever want to disregard God's leading and advice in their life? This is the greatest question in the universe.

Evil Attributes

What about the adversary? What does the Bible reveal about the attributes or characteristics of satan?

1. He is the enemy of all good and the accuser of God and man (see Mt. 13:28,39; Rev. 12:9-10; Ezek. 28:11-17).
2. He is the father of lies (see Jn. 8:44).
3. He is a murderer (see Jn. 8:44).
4. He is a sower of discord (see Mt. 13:39).
5. He is an adversary (see 1 Pet. 5:8-9).
6. He was the first sinner, the first rebel, and the first to consecrate himself to self-gratification and wage war against society (see Is. 14:12-14; Ezek. 28:11-17; Rev. 12:9; 20:7-10).
7. He is cunning (see 2 Cor.2:11; 11:14; Eph. 6:11-12).
8. He is wicked (see Mt. 13:38; Jn. 8:44; 1 Jn. 3:8; 5:18).
9. He is malignant (see Lk. 8:12; 2 Cor. 4:4; 1 Pet. 5:8).
10. He is cowardly (see Jas. 4:7).
11. He is a tempter (see Mt. 4:1-11).
12. He is a thief (see Jn. 10:10).

13. He is without principle, taking advantage of individuals in their weak moments (see Mt. 4:1-11; Lk. 22:40; 2 Cor. 2:11; 11:3).
14. He is without principle, suggesting the use of right things in a wrong way and at a wrong time (see Mt. 4:1-11).
15. He is a slanderer of God to man and man to God (see Gen. 3:1-4; Job 1:10-11; 2:1-5).
16. He appears as a deceptive angel of light (see 2 Cor. 11:14).
17. He deludes his followers regarding their eternal end (see 2 Thess. 2:8-12; Rev. 12:9; 20:7-10).
18. He is proud and deceitful (see Ezek. 28:17; 1 Tim. 3:6; Rev. 12:9).
19. He is fierce and cruel (see Lk. 8:29; 9:39).
20. He is aggressive (see Eph. 4:26-27; 6:11-18).

Satan has never been known to be merciful, good, loving, kind, gentle, pitiful, patient, or to have any of the graces of God since he became the enemy of God and man. In Scripture, he is compared to a fowler, a wolf, a thief, a serpent, and a dragon (Ps. 91:3; Jn. 10:12; 10:10; Rev. 12:9; 20:2; 12:3-9).

As we compare these two lists of attributes, it is readily evident who causes sickness, strife, and all manner of suffering in the human race. Sin and disobedience to God were introduced by him. Understand, the devil is not a negative god; rather, he is a fallen angel. He did not become more powerful as a result of the fall.

The Works of Darkness

However, if we cooperate with him, his power in our lives becomes great, and we become weakened. Sin always weakens whatever it touches. We are always weaker after we have sinned. This is why toying with disobedience is so dangerous and destructive in the life of a believer. Sin causes us to become weak vessels. Some of the works of the devil are:

1. He deceives all men (see 2 Cor. 11:14; Rev. 12:9; 20:1-10).
2. He exercised the power of death until Christ conquered death, hell, and the grave (see Heb. 2:14; Rev. 1:18).
3. He is the leader of all sinners and backsliders of the human race and all rebels against God (see 1 Jn. 3:8-10; 1 Tim. 5:15; Mt. 9:34; Eph. 6:11-12).
4. He causes all sickness, disease, and physical and mental maladies in the human race (see Lk. 13:16; Acts 10:38).
5. He tempts humankind (see Mk. 1:13; 1 Cor. 7:5).
6. He provokes men to sin (see 1 Chron. 21:1).
7. He causes offense (sec Mt. 16:23).
8. He transforms himself into an angel of light (see 2 Cor. 11:14).
9. He resists others (see Zech. 3:1-2).
10. He enters into union with others against God (see Lk. 22:3; Jn. 13:2).
11. He sends messengers to defeat saints (see 2 Cor. 12:7).
12. He hinders the gospel (see Acts 13:10; 1 Thess. 2:18).
13. He steals the Word of God from mankind lest they believe it (see Mt. 13:19; Lk. 8:12).
14. He works miracles (see 2 Thess. 2:9).
15. He contends with messengers of God in an effort to hold them captive (see Dan. 10:12-21; Jude 9).
16. He hinders answers to prayer (see Dan. 10:12-21).
17. He sets snares for men to fall into sin (see 1 Tim. 3:7; 2 Tim. 2:26).
18. He causes doublemindedness (see Jas. 1:5-9).
19. He causes doubt and unbelief (see Gen. 3:4-5; Rom. 14:23).
20. He causes darkness and oppression (see 2 Cor.4:4; 2 Pct. 1:4-9).

21. He causes deadness and weakness (see Heb. 6:1; 9:14).
22. He causes delay and compromise (see Acts 24:25; 26:28).
23. He causes division and strife (see 1 Cor. 3:1-3; 1 Pet. 5:8).
24. He makes war on the saints (see Eph. 6:10-18).

First John 3:8 says: "...For this purpose the Son of God was manifested, that He might destroy the works of the devil." As believers we have victory over the works of the devil because Jesus made them of no effect. God will never stoop so low as to use any of the works of the devil to deal with His children. I am grieved every time I hear a person say, *"God made me sick to humble me,"* or *"God caused my financial problems to teach me how to depend on Him."* God would not have sent Jesus to destroy the works of the devil only to pick them up to use on those He loves. We can have confidence that God has enough wisdom and goodness to deal with us on a higher level than the devil's. Satan *drives* us, but God *draws* us.

God Draws

I remember visiting an older gentleman a few years ago who had been very ill for a long time. He was not a member of my church, but he asked me to come and pray for him. As I began to pray, he started to weep uncontrollably. I could not console him so first I prayed for the peace of God to calm his spirit. Finally, he was able to share his concerns with me. He said he thought that God hated him. *"I did so many bad things when I was younger and God keeps making me sick to punish me down here so that I will be good enough to go to Heaven."*

This man was not only quite depressed, but he had also received some incorrect teaching about how God operates. "God doesn't even want me in His Heaven" he said, blinking back tears. "I'm not good enough." My heart went out to this man because I knew that he was expressing the feelings of so many Christians in the Body of Christ. I explained that God does not have to resort to satan's tactics to *drive* us to Him. Satan *drives* us, but God *draws* us with His love.

We must always remember that God never causes pain, problems, and persecution in our life. We experience these things because we live in a fallen world. Rather, God uses these circumstances as His opportunity to draw us to Him. If we find ourselves attributing acts of satan to God, our prayer should be:

Lord help me to know You better. Even though satan's power is great, the power of God is even greater, and as a believer, that power lives in me. Help me to recognize who satan is and how he works. I take authority over satan and cancel every assignment he has for my life. Lord, I thank You for the victory I have over the works of the devil. Amen.

Chapter 4

SATAN'S METHOD OF OPERATION

The thief cometh not, but for to steal, and to kill,
and to destroy: I am come that they might have life,
and that they might have it more abundantly.
John 10:10

SATAN IS a busy fellow. We know that he is referred to as a "thief" in Scripture. However, the adversary is not just any old thief. Most thieves only do one thing—steal. Satan is a thief who not only steals, but he also kills and destroys. Satan is not only *looking* for whom he may devour, he is *seeking*. To *seek* means "to search for diligently."

Satan is on a quest and a mission. He stakes out his prey, slithers and sloths about like a ravenous mountain lion, and then at the first opportune time, he strikes. The devil pounces on his victim and pillages and plunders every available area of the believer's life.

Satan is not out to disrupt you or upset you. His intent is to *devour* you. When something is devoured, it is utterly consumed. It is swallowed up and completely destroyed. Satan's plan for your life will never change; only his tactics and method of operation will change.

Satan's Agenda

The devil has an agenda or a plan for your life. His program is tailor-made to defeat you and hinder you in your walk with the Lord. He does not carry out his wicked work by blind chance or probability. His agenda is carefully conceived, well-planned, and systematic. Since his goal is to steal, kill, and destroy, his tactics must be carefully designed to meet that goal. His ultimate goal is to oppose the plan of God in your life. However, satan must have your permission and your cooperation in order to do so.

In the first 18 verses of John 10, Jesus likens Himself to a good shepherd. He is a good shepherd who loves and cares for His sheep. He defends them and, if necessary, He lays down His life for them. At night, sheep were often gathered into a sheepfold to protect them from thieves, weather, and wild animals. Sheepfolds were caves, sheds, or open areas surrounded by walls made of stones or branches. The shepherd often slept in the fold to protect the sheep. Just as a shepherd cares for his sheep, Jesus, the good shepherd, cares for those who follow Him. The prophet Ezekiel, in predicting the coming of the Messiah, called Him a shepherd.

> *And I will set up one shepherd over them, and he shall feed them, even My servant David; he shall feed them, and he shall be their shepherd* (Ezekiel 34:23).

Satan's agenda is to act as the thief who comes to spoil every area of our lives. In contrast to the thief who takes, Jesus gives. A hired man tends the sheep for money, while Jesus, our good Shepherd, does it for love. The shepherd owns the sheep and is committed to them. Jesus is not merely doing a job; He is committed to love us and even laid down His life for us.

The Nature of the Thief

To *steal* means "to take something from someone without their permission, in a surreptitious or a sneaky, dishonest manner." Not all thievery is the same however. There are degrees and gradations of stealing. Satan tailors his methods of operation in order to carry out his wicked deeds. There are three types of theft:

1. Robbery
2. Larceny
3. Embezzlement

Robbery

Robbery is "the taking of an individual's property off of their person by the use of threat, violence, or force." Robbery is considered a violent crime.

Larceny

Larceny, on the other hand, is not considered a violent crime. *Larceny* is "the taking of someone's property without their knowledge." Although it is a serious crime it is not considered a violent crime because the victim experiences no bodily harm.

Embezzlement

The form of theft that does the greatest harm is embezzlement. *Embezzlement* is "theft involving a breach of trust." The embezzler steals a little bit at a time. In robbery, the thief gets the loot all at one time and then tries to get away. However, an embezzler pilfers his victim's property little by little, one item at a time. People with a great deal of power embezzle.

Criminals get less prison time for embezzlement because it is considered a white-collar crime.

Satan is an embezzler. He wears us down little by little. He sends trouble and strife into our life and chips away at our trust and confidence in God. He embezzles our joy and hope and eats away at our enthusiasm. Satan can work so slowly, secretly, and methodically that you can be totally unaware that he is operating in your life.

When satan steals it is not a one-time event. Rather, it is a process. For example, when a person backslides and leaves the church, it does not happen all at once. Backsliding is not an event; it is a process. You do not lose anything in your relationship with God all at once. You lose a little bit at a time, storm by storm, trial by trial, and test by test. Every failure to develop Christ-like characteristics after a difficult test or trial will most likely result in damage to your relationship with God.

Satan wears us down and chips away at our attitude. He robs us of our fellowship and relationship with God and His people. I have seen many people, who were otherwise strong in the Lord, fall away from God and the church because they encountered a storm or suffered some great disappointment in their life that caused them to lose faith and hope. They found themselves staying away from church, praying less, and neglecting the study of God's Word altogether. They made excuses for staying away from church: "I'm going through some things now; I'll be back when I get myself together." Once again, satan blew up a few balloons to celebrate the downfall of another child of God.

In the natural realm it is impossible to stop a thief once he has made up his mind to victimize you. Burglar alarms, elaborate security systems, and booby traps will help. However, if a thief is determined to steal from you, where there is a *will* there will be a *way*. We will all be a victim of satan at one time or another. Evil is ever present in this world.

You cannot stop a thief, but you can slow down his process or protect yourself in such a way that when he strikes, his blows will not be as damaging. God has given us a spiritual *security system*, so we can feel safe from satan's attacks.

The Believer's Security System

In the natural realm, one's chances of being robbed are diminished by installing a security system and placing bright lights around the outside of a home. I live in a sparsely populated, suburban neighborhood with many trees and shrubs surrounding the widely spaced homes. There are many places for a robber to hide and creep around. All thieves, however, hate light. So my neighbors and I all have bright floodlights illuminating our driveways, walkways, and rear patio areas. The light does not guarantee that a thief won't strike, but his crime will be much more difficult to perpetrate because of the threat of exposure.

Even so, in the spirit realm the light of God's Word makes us less likely to be the victim of the thief. What can easily happen in darkness is almost impossible in the light. The believer's security system has three elements:

1. Light
2. A secure place
3. Checks and balances.

Light

Jesus called Himself the "Light of the world."

As long as I am in the world, I am the light of the world (John 9:5).

Then spake Jesus again unto them, saying, I am the light of the world: he that followeth Me shall not walk in darkness, but shall have the light of life (John 8:12).

In Him was life; and the life was the light of men (John 1:4).

Jesus Christ was the Creator of life, and His life brings light. We learn of His life through the reading and study of God's Word. In His light, we see ourselves as we really are—sinners in need of a Savior.

When we follow Jesus, the Light, we can avoid walking blindly and falling into sin. Jesus lights the path ahead of us so that we can see how to live. The truth of God's Word keeps us from stumbling. It is our guide. "Thy word is a lamp unto my feet, and a light unto my path" (Ps. 119:105).

The Word of God helps us to understand satan's ways. In the Word, we clearly see his tactics and strategies throughout the ages. Not only are his tactics exposed, but we are given instructions on how to combat his schemes in order to overcome them. The light of the gospel shining into our darkened world is like the bursting forth of the sun in the darkness.

For God, who commanded the light to shine out of darkness, hath shined in our hearts, to give the light of the knowledge of the glory of God in the face of Jesus Christ (2 Corinthians 4:6).

I avoided many pitfalls in my own life because my knowledge of God's Word and a similar situation in the Bible enabled me to be forewarned, thus avoiding a disastrous pitfall. If we keep our spiritual lives illuminated by the Word, we will be less likely to be a victim of the thief. When God said "Let there be light" in Genesis 1:3, He announced to the devil "I'm here." The first thing that God always does before He works in any situation is to turn on the light. Peter was in prison, but before God brought him out, he turned on the light in the prison.

And, behold, the angel of the Lord came upon him, and a light shined in the prison: and he smote Peter on the side, and raised him up...And his chains fell off from his hands (Acts 12:7).

The devil knows that God is life and light, so he tries to keep us in spiritual darkness. For as long as we are in the dark, we are at a disadvantage. *Darkness is the devil's habitat.*

A Secure Place

Not only do thieves hate light, they hate secure places as well. In the natural, the more secure you make your property the less likely you are to become the victim of a thief because thieves do not travel with extensive tools. It is good to have bars on your windows because most thieves do not travel with welding materials. You are safer if you have dead bolt locks on your doors because most thieves do not take the time to pick locks. The more things you do to secure your property, the less likely you are to become a victim.

It is the same way with your spiritual life. The more you guard your relationship with God by maintaining a consistent prayer life, attending church regularly, cultivating healthy relationships with other believers, and studying God's Word, the less likely you are to become a victim. You are securing what God has given you.

Many of us take what God has given us for granted, and we treat it carelessly. You must guard your anointing and your spiritual life. You cannot stop a thief, but if you leave the door open, the windows up, and announce that you are not home by leaving four or five newspapers piled on the front step, you are literally inviting a thief to come in and take your belongings.

However, when the would-be thief sees a lot of light and bars on the windows, a security door, and a guard dog in the front yard, he will think twice before he hits your house.

Those kinds of things are a tremendous deterrent in our spiritual lives as well. When the enemy begins to pounce and to steal from you what God has given you, he will see that you are a prayer warrior and a Bible believer. When he does, he will back off from you and think twice.

Checks and Balances

Satan specializes in embezzlement. The only way to guard against embezzlement is to have a system of checks and balances. In the natural world, one must have a system of checks and balances in order to keep people from stealing from you. If the same person who collects the money also writes the receipt, then takes the money to the bank, records it, and balances the book—that is a dangerous situation. The reason the devil escapes with so many of our belongings is because we often do not have a system of checks and balances.

God has established a system of checks and balances for us. It is found in the spiritual oversight and Christian fellowship we have with others in the church. When we do not have the spiritual care of a pastor, we have no one to put us back on track if we get off course. A Bible-believing, Christ-centered church provides us with a measuring stick wherewith we can monitor our own growth and maturity in God. To neglect Christian meetings is to give up the encouragement and help of other Christians.

And let us consider one another to provoke unto love and to good works: not forsaking the assembling of ourselves together, as the manner of some is; but exhorting one another: and so much the more, as ye see the day approaching (Hebrews 10:24-25).

We gather together to share our faith and to strengthen one another in the Lord. As we get closer to the day when Christ returns, we will face many spiritual struggles and persecution. Difficulties should never be excuses for missing church services. Rather, as difficulties arise, we should make an even greater effort to be faithful in attendance.

Subtle Assaults

In these days, men and women are interested in anything that appears attractive. We are living in an age of glitzy advertisements, and people are ready to believe almost anything. They believe what they read, what other people tell them, and what they see on television. They also believe what they see in our lives.

Therefore, it is reasonable to believe that if others see a life of joy, happiness, and triumph in us, they will be anxious to discover the secret of such success. So often Christians give the impression that they are dejected and depressed. They send a message to others that says, "Accepting Jesus Christ means you will have even more problems."

However, we must recognize that some of us give this impression because we suffer from the depression that results from satanic attack. Unfortunately, we often grossly and grievously misrepresent the gospel of hope and redeeming grace.

Now all of this, of course, is due to the fact that we are confronted by a very powerful adversary. The fact is that the moment we become a believer in Jesus Christ we become subjected to the subtle and powerful assaults of one who is described in the Bible as "the prince of the power of the air"; "the spirit that now worketh in the children of disobedience" (Eph. 2:2); and "the god of this world."

It is wise and crucial that, as believers, we study and consider the ways the devil comes to us, attacks us, deludes us, and leads us astray without our realizing it at all. As we examine satan's method of operation and its subtlety, we begin to understand why so many fail.

We Are Not Ignorant

Satan is the most subtle and dangerous when he comes as "an angel of light" and a would-be friend of the church (2 Cor. 11:14). According to the Scriptures, he does just that, and at that point he is not subtle at all. Second Corinthians 2:11 says, "Lest Satan should get an advantage of us: for we are not ignorant of his devices."

In view of this, we must prepare ourselves for his attacks. Studying the Scriptures gives us insight and helps us to understand his methods. Although Paul states we are not ignorant of satan's devices (or, we do not need to be), *the tragedy is that so many believers are ignorant of his devices. They do not believe in his existence, and even those who do fail to remember that he is always there and that he can appear in many subtle forms.*

As I look objectively at what he does to us, I cannot help but be amazed at the utter foolishness of so many people. We have all had the experience of looking back over our own life and asking ourselves, "How could I have fallen into that trap so easily?"

In retrospect, it all seems so perfectly plain and obvious, yet we continue to make the same mistakes. This is because the devil's methods are so subtle. He makes things appear so attractive to us that we fall almost before we realize it.

I counseled a woman some years ago who was experiencing divorce for the second time. She could not understand how she had made such a poor choice not once, but twice. "My first husband was an alcoholic," she said, "and he was very abusive." She finally found the courage to take her three young children and leave but only after years of praying and struggling.

After carefully analyzing the situation and figuring out what she did wrong, she embarked on another relationship.

This time it will be different, she told herself, *He does not drink, he is not violent, and this has to work*. Less than four years after the start of the second marriage, she found herself literally right back where she started—sitting in my office angry, depressed, and wondering what went wrong.

Over the course of several weeks of counseling, this lovely young woman discovered that her second husband was very much like her first husband. "He has never hit me," she said, "and he's never taken a drink in his life." Yet further discussion and closer examination revealed that although husband number one abused her physically, husband number two abused her verbally. Both were abusive. One drank. The other showed a number of signs of self-abuse and addictive behavior. Both men had similar character flaws and emotional problems, but they manifested them in very different ways—the subtlety of satan!

The devil's methods of operation resemble an animal trap covered over with leaves and shrubs that completely conceal the danger below. If the unwitting victim could somehow sense the danger, much pain, and even death, could be avoided. Only through a lifelong, consistent study of God's Word can believers consistently uncover the traps satan has set before us. It is not God's will for us to be ignorant of satan's devices.

Co-Conspirators

Satan cannot do anything in our lives on his own. He needs our cooperation. He needs you and I as co-conspirators in order to carry out his work. A *co-conspirator* is "one who works alongside the perpetrator in complete cooperation in order to commit an illegal act." Satan needs our help. He looks for our help. If he wants to spread an evil report in the church to discredit someone's character, he must have someone to tell the lie to, someone to carry it, and someone to listen to it. If he wants to hinder the work of the church, he must have groups of people who are willing to challenge the leadership of the pastor and criticize everything the church is doing. If he wants to keep certain people from growing in Christ, those individuals must be willing to only attend church sporadically, stay away from Bible study and all instruction in the Word, and compromise their prayer life. Satan cannot operate in our lives without some form of cooperation from us. God has not given him that kind of power. The devil and all of his demons were made subject to Christ and believers by the atonement, the name of Jesus, and the Holy Spirit.

> *And these signs shall follow them that believe; In My name shall they cast out devils; they shall speak with new tongues* (Mark 16:17).

King David was his own worst enemy, especially when it came to resisting satan in his life. When he sinned with Bathsheba, satan needed David's full cooperation in order to successfully lure him into that sin. David abused his position of authority to get what he wanted. His personal life became entangled in sin. He committed adultery with Bathsheba and then ordered her husband to be killed in an attempt to cover it up. He sinned deliberately and conspired with satan to carry out his act of immorality, deception, and finally murder.

A Way to Escape

Satan's plan for our life will never change. His eternal goal is to hinder God's plan for each one of us. However, God's Word encourages us:

> *There hath no temptation taken you but such as is common to man: but God is faithful, who will not suffer you to be tempted above that ye are able; but will with the temptation also make a way to escape, that ye may be able to bear it* (1 Corinthians 10:13).

This verse of Scripture assures us of the eternal keeping power of God and help in all temptations, providing we obey the warnings. No one can be kept from a fall if he persistently refuses to meet conditions. Our standing depends upon our faith and union with God and our steadfastness in prayer. The greatest saint can stand only as long as he or she depends upon God and continues in obedience to the gospel.

Run, Don't Walk

Running away or shunning something is sometimes considered cowardly. However, wise people realize that removing themselves physically from temptation is often the most courageous action to take. Knowing *when to run* is as important in spiritual battle as knowing *when and how to fight*. No matter how subtle and cunning satan's methods of operation are, knowing God's Word and running from a tempting situation is the first step to victory.

Paul warned Timothy, a young man in ministry, to shun anything that produced evil thoughts:

Flee also youthful lusts: but follow righteousness, faith, charity, peace, with them that call on the Lord out of a pure heart (2 Timothy 2:22).

In a culture filled with depravity and pressures, satan has many avenues and channels through which to work. Still, we should be encouraged that, no matter how great the attacks of the enemy, the power of God to keep and deliver us is even greater. God's Word says, "...greater is He that is in you, than he that is in the world (1 Jn. 4:4).

Remember

1. Temptation happens to everyone, so do not feel as though you have been singled out.
2. Others have resisted satan and so can you.

3. Any temptation can be resisted because God will help you to resist it.

God Helps You Resist Temptation

1. He helps you to recognize those people and situations that give you trouble.
2. He helps you to run from anything you know is wrong.
3. He helps you to choose to do only what is right.
4. He helps you to pray for His help.
5. He helps you to seek friends who love God and can offer help when you are tempted.

Once you come to an understanding of how satan works, pray this believer's prayer:

Dear Lord, create in me a sincere desire to know Your Word. Help me to be more consistent in my prayer life. Keep my spiritual eyes open so I will not become an unwilling victim of satan. Bless me that I might remain an active, interested member of a Bible-believing, Christ-centered church. Amen.

Chapter 5

Schemes and Scams/ Plots and Plans

Now the Spirit speaketh expressly,
that in the latter times some shall depart from the faith,
giving heed to seducing spirits, and doctrines of devils.
1 Timothy 4:1

THE PICTURE is etched in my brain forever. A world-renown church leader is standing before television cameras, his face twisted, eyes weeping, and he is exposing his sins and transgressions to the world. As I watched him, I felt anger, disgust, sorrow, and sympathy all at the same time. What a tragedy. Yet in these latter times, many believers will be led astray by evil spirits that seduce, deceive, and lure them away from the plan and will of God. The "latter times" began with Christ's resurrection and will continue until He returns to set up His Kingdom and judge all mankind.

Satan's Baby-Sitters

Satan is not omnipresent. Unlike God, he is not capable of being everywhere at the same time. However, he is determined to counterfeit the doctrines and experiences of God (as revealed in Scripture) and deceive believers all over the world. This is the most important work that he has to accomplish.

The task is an awesome one, and satan is not capable of carrying out this work on his own. Therefore, he has his own angels (evil, wicked spirits) who work on his behalf. They are his emissaries. The word *demon* is not found in Scripture, but it means "evil spirits or devil." The word *devil* is used for "satan, the prince of demons." He is the chief devil and the original source of evil in the universe.

There is only one "prince of devils," but there are many demons. Satan has a spirit and cannot enter the body of persons or beasts. However, demons are disembodied spirits and do not seem to be able to operate in the material world except through the possession of bodies (people or beasts).

Thousands of them can enter and take possession of one person at the same time. The demons' goal is to control the humans they inhabit. Jesus encountered a man living among the tombs in a graveyard who was possessed with many demons. The demons caused the man to physically abuse himself. When they saw Jesus afar off, they recognized Him and feared Him. Jesus spoke to the demonic presence in the man and asked him to name himself. "And He asked him, What is thy name? And he answered, saying, My name is Legion: for we are many" (Mk. 5:9).

Demon *possession* and demon *influence* are different. A believer cannot be possessed by a demon. *Possession* means "the state of being dominated." The Holy Spirit is the unmerited gift of God to all believers. The Holy Spirit and a demonic spirit cannot indwell a person at the same time. Yet, as believers, we certainly can experience *oppression*, *depression*, and *suppression* by evil spirits. Our only resources against them are prayer, self-control, and the whole armor of God.

The Mystery of Iniquity

Paul writes to Timothy, his closest companion, and gives him practical advice about discipline in the Christian life. He warns him about the "last day" danger and the condition that the church will be in near the time of Jesus Christ's return. "Some," he says, "will give in to seducing or enticing spirits" (see 1 Tim. 4:1).

Seduce means "to lead away, especially away from the path of right or virtue." When one is seduced, one is led on an evil and disastrous course. Seducing spirits are emissaries of satan. They are mysterious in their work and efforts to lead people away from God. These spirits are everywhere and their forces and influences have increased in these latter days.

Again, these demonic forces have no physical body. They must have a personal body to operate through. The spirit of jealousy cannot work by itself. It needs a weak, insecure person with low self-esteem to attach itself to before it can carry out its destructive path of envy and strife. A spirit of hatred and animosity cannot hang around in the atmosphere and work on its own. It must attach itself to someone who does not have the love of Christ and the sweet communion of the Holy Spirit within him.

It is almost as if there are groupings of demons armed with a fistful of scams, schemes, plots, and plans designed to infiltrate and wreak havoc in the house of God. These spiritual workers of iniquity probably never show up at Bible study or Sunday school where teaching is taking place. If they do, it is only to bring a spirit of distraction and confusion. They come in large numbers to Sunday morning worship service. They influence people to criticize the singing and the praisers with comments like "It doesn't take all that" and "Some people are too emotional."

It is almost as if there are evil spirits specifically assigned to hinder worship in any way that they possibly can. If possible, they cause people to feel sleepy or bored when the preaching of the Word comes forth. They attempt to interfere with the offering by reminding us of unpaid bills, things we want to buy, and vacations we want to take. Satan celebrates and hell is happy whenever the work and worship of God is hindered.

Familiar Spirits

With God's permission (see the discussion of Job in Chapter 1), satan assigns carefully selected evil spirits to your life. These evil spirits know how to defeat you and make your life miserable. They know what it takes to make you feel rejected, inadequate, fearful, unhappy, unfulfilled, and defeated. They are *familiar* with you. They become familiar with you by living with you and around you, and they use their knowledge of you to bring defeat into your life.

Satan knows your weak areas and concentrates his efforts there. Satan is not smart; he is just knowledgeable and consistent. Mohammed Ali was not the smartest boxer that ever entered a ring, but he was certainly knowledgeable and consistent. He familiarized himself with his opponent. He studied his moves, especially his weak areas. Then Mohammed Ali tailor-made his moves to target those weak areas. If the opponent had a good left jab, but he tired easily, Ali would spend much time jumping and dancing about in an effort to tire his opponent out. He targeted his opponent's weak areas and it worked. Time and time again he scored a "knock out" that was based on his skill and ability but was based even more on his knowledge and familiarity with his opponent.

Satan opposes us in much the same way. He targets those areas where we tend to be the most sensitive and vulnerable. For example, if you are a family-centered, family-oriented person who sees your loved ones and family life as a source of joy and fulfillment, then the familiar spirits around you will most likely attack you in that area. When satan attacks the home and marriage, he targets the weakest link. An attack in any other area would not be as devastating.

If you are very particular about your appearance and physical health and you are devastated by the least little dysfunction or alteration, then familiar spirits will attack you in that area. If gossip hurts you, then those familiar spirits will cause others to scandalize and discredit your good name. Familiar spirits are aware of your vulnerabilities and will seek to defeat you in your weak areas.

A Devil at Every Level

The powers of darkness are highly organized. Every rebel spirit that opposes God has an operational level to carry out its evil assignment. There are four kinds of rebel spirits. These devils work at every level of human existence to foster evil.

1. There are *principalities*, which are chief rulers or beings of the highest rank and order in satan's kingdom (see Eph. 6:12; 1:21; Col. 2:10).
2. There are *authorities*, which derive their power from and execute the will of the chief rulers (see Eph. 6:12; 1:21; Col. 2:10).
3. There are *spirit world-rulers*, which rule the darkness of this age (see Dan. 10:12-21; Eph. 1:21; 6:12; Col. 1:16).
4. There are *wicked spirits*, which dwell in the heavenlies (Eph. 6:12; 1:21; Col. 1:16).

There are demon spirits for every sickness, unholy trait, evil behavior, wicked plan, and doctrinal error known among men. Even disease germs, which are closely allied with unclean spirits, are really living forms of corruption that enter the bodies of people and bring them to death. Just as garbage and trash breeds maggots, so humankind (in the fallen state of corruption) breeds evil through unclean living and contact with corruption. Germs are agents of satan, corrupting the bodies of victims.

The evidence of demonic activity can be observed in every arena and strata of life. The presence of the influence of evil can be seen in the church, the lives of individual believers, homes, marriages, communities, nations, and the world at large. No area of life is immune from satanic harassment.

Satan in the Church

Perhaps the most disturbing example of this phenomena is the subtle influence of evil in the church and the lives of individual believers. The devil's strategy for believers is to lead them astray and deceive them. Believers are deceived or drawn into evil (especially to entice, to surrender charity, compromise values, forfeit virtue, and forsake integrity).

The first work of demons is to urge a *departure from the faith*. This results in departure from holy living and acceptance of doctrines that will damn the soul. I have often observed this departure from the faith in the lives of believers in the church. If we are not careful, each of us can fall victim to the subtle scheming of the adversary.

In the church, satan lures certain individuals through the promise of power. Most pastors, at some time or another, have had to confront a church officer whose misguided notion of his position caused him or her to challenge leadership. Satan uses wayward deacons and renegade associate ministers in a church to oppose God's plan that has been given to the pastor.

I am reminded of a time when our church, with the leading of the Holy Spirit, organized and carried out a building fund effort. I searched the Word of God to make sure that the project was based upon and carried out upon biblical principles. For several months I preached sermons and taught Bible study lessons focused upon what God says about building His house. As a church family, we decided to plant financial seeds in our building fund instead of selling dinners, chances, and raffle tickets to support God's program.

Several church leaders, along with a few associate ministers, formed an alliance to resist this effort because they did not want to give their money. They went through the congregation quietly murmuring and planting seeds of doubt in the minds of others. The devil was determined to see our building fund effort fail, but I was determined to do God's work in God's way. I recognized the enemy's plan and designed a strategy to oppose it.

After much prayer and fasting, the Lord spoke to me and said, "*Build My people and I will build the church.*" I followed God's instructions. I did not disfellowship those church members, nor did I discipline them immediately. Instead, I continued to teach and preach the Word of God. I talked about how the Lord utterly destroyed the rebellious Israelites in Numbers 16 when they openly disobeyed Moses leadership. I talked about how the people of God were instructed to give their money for the building of the Temple in First Chronicles 29. I preached and taught God's Word concerning the matter, and in due time the devils began to scatter. The building fund program suceeded, and the church moved forward as a result.

Splinter Groups

Satan attempts to divide the church at every level. He seeks to cause division by encouraging *splinter groups*, organized around a common gripe or shared grievance. A subchurch within the church soon emerges with a ring leader that I call the "little pastor." These little pastors are planted in every local church and act as vision destroyers and ministry saboteurs. They are pharisees because they are usually in some type of leadership position. They look, act, and sound religious, but ultimately they seek to bring division and destruction.

Satan encourages them to scam, scheme, plot, and plan to subtly oppose everything that the pastor tries to do to build the ministry. Satan plants his helpers in the choir, the youth ministry, the evangelism team, the trustee ministry, the deacon ministry, the missionary ministry, and wherever else he can find willing vessels who will allow him to work through them.

Whenever the fellowship in a church is destroyed, it does not happen as a result of outside influences. When the love, trust, and fellowship in the Body of Christ is hindered, seducing spirits are working on the inside to cause the spiritual and emotional collapse of God's people.

Satan seeks to cause *implosion*. *Explosion* is "a violent outburst that causes everything to scatter outward," but *implosion* is "a violent collapse inward." Churches have split and divided; some have closed their doors due to the internal strife and endless fighting. Sometimes disgruntled members walk away mad and start new churches that are not sanctioned by God. These *man houses* are not houses of God, but they are places where satan can continue to carry out his plan of destruction.

Satan has succeeded by causing some believers to think that one group is more special to God than another. Religious organizations have divided and created new denominations based on a few minor individual differences and preferences not a fundamental difference in doctrine or principle. What starts out as a dislike for a certain type of clothing or dress gets perverted and spiritualized into a dogma that creates division and separation.

It seems silly now, but there was a time when some people felt they could not hear from God effectively with a pair of earrings on their ears. They thought they could not "get a prayer through" wearing lipstick. I remember being ostracized by other Christians for years for wearing lipstick in church. We may laugh at the foolishness of such narrow-mindedness now, but it was not funny then. If satan can get us to major on such minor things, division disrupts the fellowship. Hell rejoices and satan celebrates when God's people become divided and the vision of a ministry does not move forward.

Another One Bites the Dust

An old rock and roll song, made popular many years ago, contained the euphemism, "bite the dust." It was a colloquial way of saying that someone had failed or missed the mark. We bite the dust every time we end up groveling on the ground, defeated by the plots and plans levied against us by the devil.

Every year we hear stories about a brother or sister falling victim to sin and the destruction of their ministry. In the Body of Christ the preacher is crucial because he or she is the vessel that carries the Word of God. Faith comes by hearing and hearing by the preaching of the Word (see Rom. 10:17). Satan knows that if the preacher does not preach the Word, we cannot hear, believe, or respond in faith.

Therefore, the adversary designs a plan to lure the preacher into sin and cause him or her to live a compromised life. I am grieved every time I hear reports about a preacher caught in sin and any form of immorality. I am even more distressed when a preacher refuses to acknowledge the sin, as if God's standards for him or her are different because of the call to ministry. No matter how powerful we preach, no matter how many souls we lead to Christ, God still holds us individually responsible for our decisions and behavior.

Satan's goal in the lives of preachers and teachers who carry the Word is not to *destroy* them, but to *defile* them, *pollute* their message, and *render them ineffective* as mouthpieces for God. The devil blinds the preacher to the truth of the direct connection between the preacher's walk and his talk. The greatest sermon the preacher preaches is the life he or she lives on a day-to-day basis. Satan knows that every time one pastor is found in sin *many* people are affected. In other words, when the leader falls or goes astray, those who follow will scatter. The Lord said through His prophet: "...smite the shepherd, and the sheep shall be scattered" (Zech. 13:7b).

I watched a dear friend succumb to the subtle schemes of the enemy. Satan crept up on his *blind side* and successfully destroyed his marriage, his family, and eventually his ministry as pastor of a well-established Pentecostal church. The demon was alcohol. What started out as a "night-cap" to help him unwind after a long day in the Lord's service soon became alcoholism—with all of its evils and devastation.

How subtle the enemy was! The saddest part of the story is that I went to my friend many times to warn him and share my feelings with him concerning what he was doing to himself. He refused to listen. Satan had blinded him to his own behavior. No one else would talk to him about his behavior because he was the "pastor," and pastors do not have these kinds of problems. If they do, you certainly do not point it out to them.

With much pain and anguish I watched my dear friend and comrade utterly destroy everything God had given him. The good news is that even when we fall, even when we bite the dust, we can dust ourselves off and get up again.

Try Again

When we fall prey to satan's schemes and scams, he rejoices, but God says to us, "Try again." Unlike a driver's test, when we make a mistake or miss a turn, God does not say, "Stop, pull over, get out, and give up the keys." Instead, God says "Back up, get your bearings, chart your course, and try again." If you have ever fallen victim to the adversary, there are three things you can do to guard against victimization again. Remember:

1. Satan imitates God's voice.
2. Satan seeks to attract your attention away from God.
3. Satan has a counterfeit for whatever God offers.

You can overcome past failures. While satan is keeping a record of your past failures, God is scheduling your future victories. Jesus warns us of trouble and tribulation, but He also encourages us in the midst of it. "...In the world ye shall have tribulation: but be of good cheer; I have overcome the world" (Jn. 16:33).

If you have been or are presently experiencing difficulty in any area of your life as a result of demonic activity, God wants you to be set free. As believers, we do not need to give heed to seducing spirits. God gives us power to be overcomers. In order to cancel satan's plans for our life we must:

1. Reject all negative feedback.
2. Listen to the Holy Spirit.
3. Consult with the Father.

Reject All Negative Feedback

We must understand that evil spirits can bring negative influences upon us by feeding negative comments into our spirits. This breeds fear, doubt, and defeat. Jesus did not give the same quality time to the Pharisees that He gave to the Samaritan woman. Sometimes negative feedback comes from other people influenced by satan to harm you. Jesus discerned the *purpose* of every conversation, whether it came from a hungry heart or a critical attitude.

Refuse to release words of defeat, depression, and discouragement. Your words are life. Express hope and confidence in God. You must understand the power of words. Get so excited over planning your triumphs that you do not have time to complain over past losses. Never speak words that make satan think he is winning.

Listen to the Holy Spirit

Eliminate the time-wasters in your life. Concentrate on your God-connection. Listen to the Holy Spirit. The voice of God speaks loudly and clearly through His Word. Read it. Study it. Evaluate it. Digest it. Live it.

Consult With the Father

There is no substitute for open, honest communication with God. I believe that God wants us to be *straight up* with him. In other words, when we encounter an attack from satan that leaves us feeling angry, rejected, and helpless, God wants us to share those feelings with Him.

Prayer can be a time of purging for us. Through the Word and private prayer time, we discover God's plan for us. Usually it is revealed step by step. The more aware you are of God's plan for your life, the more readily you will be able to distinguish it from the evil plans of satan. Pray this believer's prayer:

Lord, help me to be aware of satanic devices. Help me to guard my spiritual life. When I make a mistake, remind me that Your love is unconditional and that I can always try again. Amen.

Chapter 6

MY PEOPLE PERISH

*My people are destroyed for lack of knowledge: because
thou hast rejected knowledge, I will also reject thee, that
thou shalt be no priest to me: seeing thou hast forgotten
the law of thy God, I will also forget thy children.*
Hosea 4:6

THE DEVIL'S most incredible feat has been to convince the world that he does not exist. Satan is the father of lies. He is shrewd in his operation. He is cunning and crafty, and he delights in deception. John 8:44 says, "...for he a liar, and the father of it."

Don't Buy the Lie

When satan told Adam and Eve that they could partake of the forbidden fruit—he was lying. When he told Lot he could pitch his tent toward Sodom—he was lying. When he told Saul he could consult with the witch of Endor—he was lying. When he told David he could sleep with Bathsheba—he was lying. Satan lied to Noah, Abraham, Moses, Joseph, Gideon, Esther, Deborah, Hannah, and he lies to us too. There is no truth in him.

There are two equal and opposite errors into which our race can fall about devils and demons. One is to disbelieve in their existence. The other is to believe, and to feel an excessive and unhealthy interest in them.

Satan feeds upon sin and our own ignorance of him. Any area of your heart or mind that is not surrendered to Jesus Christ is an area that is vulnerable to satanic attack. Wherever there is a habit of sin in a believer's life, expect to find demonic activity in that area. The sin-habit often becomes the dwelling place or habitation (stronghold) for a spirit. That spirit robs a believer of power and joy.

Many believers have been taught that once they are saved and have the Holy Spirit, they cannot be deceived. Tragically, this is not true. It is so easy to fall into self-deception. This is one reason the Spirit of Truth was sent. In fact, the very *thought* that a Christian cannot be deceived is, in itself, a deception. Once that particular *lie* permeates a believer's mind, his ideas and opinions crystallize and he remains in his present state of spiritual immaturity. All manner of spirits will attack the soul, knowing they are protected by the armor of that person's own thoughts and doctrines. Christians can be *oppressed, suppressed, and depressed by demons* that can occupy unregenerate thought systems. This is especially true if those thoughts are defended by self-deception or false doctrines.

The thought, *I cannot have a demon because I am a Christian*, is simply not true. Do not buy the lie! A demon cannot have you in an eternal possessive sense, but *you can have a demon* if you refuse to repent of your sympathetic thoughts toward evil. It is quite difficult to break the power of religious self-deception. The very nature of *faith* does not give room for doubt.

Once a person is deceived, he does not recognize that he is deceived because he has been deceived! For all that we think we know, we must accept this as well—we can be wrong. If we refuse to accept this truth, how will we ever be corrected from our errors?

Casting Down Imaginations

Any area of our heart or mind that is not surrendered to Jesus Christ is vulnerable to satanic attack. It is here in the uncrucified thought-life of the believer's mind that the pulling down of strongholds is of vital importance.

You may not agree with the idea that evil spirits can frequent and occupy attitudes in a believer's life, but you must certainly agree that each one of us has a carnal mind and that the carnal mind is a source of vain imaginations and thoughts that exalt themselves above God.

Casting down imaginations, and every high thing that exalteth itself against the knowledge of God, and bringing into captivity every thought to the obedience of Christ (2 Corinthians 10:5).

We deal with the devil by dealing with carnal thought systems, the strongholds that protect the adversary. For this reason, we must attain *humility of mind* before real deliverance is possible. When we discover rebellion toward God within us, we must not defend or excuse ourselves. Rather, we must humble our hearts and repent, exercising our faith in God to change us.

Commander-in-Chief

We, like Paul, are merely weak humans, but we do not need to use human plans and methods to win our battles.

God's mighty weapons are available to us as we fight against satan's strongholds. The Christian must choose whose weapons to use, God's or man's. Paul assures us that we have God's mighty weapons:

1. Prayer
2. Faith
3. Hope
4. Love
5. God's Word
6. The Holy Spirit

These weapons are powerful and effective (see Eph. 6:13-18). They can break down the proud human arguments against God as well as the walls satan builds to keep people from finding God. When dealing with the pride that keeps people from a relationship with Christ, we may be tempted to use our own methods. Yet nothing can break down these barriers like God's weapons. Paul uses military terminology to describe this warfare against sin and satan. He says, "...we do not war after the flesh: (For the weapons of our warfare are not carnal...)" (2 Cor. 10:3-4).

God must be our *Commander-in Chief*. Even our thoughts must submit to His control as we live for Him. We destroy reasonings of pagan philosophies and dogmas that nullify the Word of God and the facts of the gospel. We pull down these fortifications and demolish them. We put the demon powers and alien armies to flight as we raise high the cross of Christ on every spiritual battlefield. We demolish all theories, reasonings, and any high system of ethics, religion, mythology, metaphysics, sublime doctrines, or philosophy set forth to defy the knowledge of God. We bring every thought *prisoner* and lead it into captivity to obey Christ. Lascivious, vain, and evil thoughts of all kinds are brought down and made obedient to

His laws. This includes any thinking that is contrary to virtue, purity, and righteousness.

Already, A Defeated Foe

God does not condemn those who fall, only those who *lay there*. Consider Job, the king of bad circumstances. Job was a man who had everything and lost it all. All he had left was a complaining, faithless wife, a painful disease, and a circle of three condemning friends. The attacks of satan were so devastating and far-reaching in his life that Job could have given up; but I like what he said in Job 17:9: "The righteous also shall hold on his way, and he that hath clean hands shall be stronger and stronger."

This means that no matter how severe the attack, the righteous do not give up. Some believers give up because they do not realize that satan is *already a defeated foe*. However, he has already lost the struggle between good and evil. God is victorious!

We are God's, and we share in that eternal victory. The same power that conquered death and raised Jesus from the dead is resident in us. Sometimes we limit God by our *tiny* image of Him. Satan wants us believe that past failures, sins, and transgressions will forever inhibit our growth and usefulness to God. However, you must understand satan's true position. He is down and he is out, already a defeated foe!

Looking Back at the Past

Some people are crippled as a result of looking back, not to some particular sin, but to the fact that they were so late in coming into the Kingdom. They are always bemoaning the fact that they have missed so many opportunities of doing good, helping others, and serving. They say, "If only I had seen all this when I was young. I would have done more for God, but it is too late now."

Missed opportunities! Some Christians become depressed by the fact that they have wasted so much time. After many long years outside the Kingdom of God, they continue to wallow in self-pity. They become so upset with thoughts of "if only" that their regret stagnates them and makes them ineffective *now*. They are simply *stuck* in the sorrow of the past.

You cannot look back across your past life without seeing things to regret. That is as it should be; but there is a fine line of distinction that lies between a legitimate regret and a wrong condition of misery and dejection that renders us ineffective.

Many times I have heard people express a fear of sharing their testimony because it speaks of a past life that is too embarrassing to talk about. Some believers never talk about the sins they were delivered from (drug addiction, alcoholism, pride, and promiscuity) or the abortions, incest, and sexual abuse in their past.

We must remember that when we have successfully waged war against satan, those experiences become a rich part of our testimony. Our testimonies help and encourage others. Satan would like nothing better than to shut the mouths of all those who have a good word to say about God. When satan reminds you of your *past*, remind him of your *future*.

Program, Deprogram, Reprogram

The past cannot be recalled, and you cannot do anything about it. The world tells us that there is "no use crying over spilt milk." Well, quote *that* one to the devil. Do not waste time and energy in vain regrets about things that you cannot change or undo. These principles remind us to move on:

1. If you cannot do anything about a situation, stop thinking about it. Never look back at it again. If you do, the devil is defeating you. Vague useless regrets must be dismissed as irrational.

2. To dwell on the past simply causes failure in the present. This cripples you and prevents you from working in the present. It is reprehensible to allow anything *that belongs to the past* to cause failure in the present.
3. If you really believe what you say about the past, then make up for it now. Give yourself entirely to living at this present moment.

If you are a Christian, it is what you are now, not what you once were, that is important. Matthew 20:1-16 gives us a perfect illustration about laborers in the vineyard who were hired at different hours of the day, some not until the eleventh hour. Some of us entered the Kingdom at the eleventh hour. Yet it is not the time of your entry into the Kingdom that matters, but the fact that you are in the Kingdom.

It is foolish to allow satan to make you mourn the fact that it was not earlier. That only robs you of things you could be enjoying now. It is like a man going to a great exhibition and discovering that there is a long line. He has come rather late. He arrives at the exhibition, but has to wait such a long time that he is almost the last one to get in.

What would you think of the man if, after entering, he simply stood at the door saying, "What a shame I wasn't the first one in. What a pity I didn't get here earlier." How silly, yet that is exactly what some of us are doing spiritually.

Those men in the twentieth chapter of Matthew were the last to enter the vineyard. It was the eleventh hour, but they were in. That's what counted. It is *being in* that matters, not when you come in, or how you come in. It is not the mode or manner of conversion that matters. What matters is that you are saved.

God has given us a method of *deprogramming* to help us to transform and renew our thinking about ourselves. Remember, the devil's playground is the mind. Satan begins his program of destruction in the mind of an individual first. If he can be defeated at that juncture, his entire program is canceled.

We can deprogram ourselves of the evil reports satan has given us by simply speaking words of encouragement to ourselves. Say this to yourself everyday:

I am what I am, whatever the past may have been. It is what I am that matters. What am I? I am forgiven. I am reconciled to God by the blood of Jesus. I am a child of God. I am adopted into God's family, and I am an heir with Christ, a joint-heir with Him. I am what I am by the grace of God.

Back to Basics

No doubt all of us would like to have a spirit sensitive enough to warn us of approaching danger and strong enough to fight it when it comes. You can have that and much more. Saying the right words or having good intentions does not count—actions do. Your spirit can be strengthened through a rigorous, diligent routine and total commitment to God's will. The moment you cease progressing, stagnation sets in.

A strong contrast exists between body and spirit. Physical fitness develops after months and years of hard work and discipline. One exercises to strengthen muscle, and one diets to lose excess fat. Then, after much effort, you enjoy increased vigor and a longer healthier life. I never realized the value and necessity of physical exercise until I started walking at least two miles every day. I have never had a weight problem, so I did not think that I had a real need to exercise. Now, after establishing the habit, if I miss one day, my entire equilibrium is affected.

The spirit must be strengthened in the same way, on a daily basis. Over the years I have practiced a morning regimen that strengthens my spirit and prepares me to face any attack the enemy has planned for me that day. I go *back to basics* with the Word of God and prayer.

1. I thank God for a peaceful night's rest.
2. I ask for guidance for the coming day.
3. I confess my sins. I receive forgiveness.
4. I declare God's Word.
5. I make my requests.
6. I sing praise songs to honor God.
7. I thank God for hearing and answering me.

Pray this believer's prayer and make a commitment to go *back to basics*:

Lord, I reject every evil report the devil sends me. I know that I am forgiven of the sins and mistakes of my past. The life I now live is my new life in Christ. Fill my mind with the knowledge of who You are and the blessings You have in store for me. Amen.

Chapter 7

DELIVER US FROM EVIL

*Yea, though I walk through the valley of the shadow of
death, I will fear no evil: for Thou art with me....*
Psalm 23:4

Perhaps no other area of Christian ministry is so widely misunderstood or studiously avoided as the "deliverance ministry." Yet many of God's people remain under heavy burdens of bondage and oppression. Before we continue, let us first understand that a demon cannot dwell in a true Christian's spirit. Through regeneration, the human spirit becomes the home of the Holy Spirit. However, as previously discussed, a believer *can* suffer oppression from demonic activity.

Many believers hide their heads in the sand of trepidation when it comes to receiving and maintaining their deliverance from the oppression of satan. They feel dread and apprehension at the very thought of having to put forth much effort to keep satan from gaining access to their lives. If you want to be successful in spiritual battle, your warfare must be waged according to the Scriptures. If you are ignorant of the need to bring Christ into the delivered soul, there is the danger of the "last state" becoming worse than the first.

Jesus said in Matthew 12:43-45 that when an unclean spirit goes out of a person, it passes through waterless places, looking for a place to rest and not finding any. Then the spirit says, "I will return to the person I came from." When it returns, it finds the person's heart clean but empty. Then the demon finds seven other spirits more evil than itself, and they all enter the person and oppress him. So the individual is worse off than before.

Christ must enter and be allowed to build His house of righteousness in the very area where satan once dwelt. God's Word gives believers clear instructions on how to maintain our deliverance from satanic oppression.

In Mark 16:17-18 there is a list of five signs that follow believers:

1. "In My name shall they cast out devils."
2. "They shall speak with new tongues."
3. "They shall take up serpents."
4. "If they drink any deadly thing, it shall not hurt them."
5. "They shall lay hands on the sick, and they shall recover."

Four of these signs have been accepted as "believer-to-believer" ministries. Yet the very first one, *casting out devils*, has been neglected.

There is factual, biblical instruction available to undergird Christian workers who recognize the need for the ministry of deliverance.

The Biblical Basis of Deliverance

There are two worlds, or realms. Both realms are real, important, and God-created. These two realms are the natural world and the spiritual world. There are only two supernatural powers or personalities—God and satan. Both desire to inhabit mankind—God for good and satan for evil. In this "contest for control," satan hates mankind and wants us bound, but God loves mankind and wants us free.

The spirit world is vastly more powerful than the natural world; the visible began in the invisible realm. Instant and complete work can be done in the spiritual world while there may be a great lapse of time before it is manifested in the natural world. A wonderful example of this phenomenon is found in Daniel chapter 10. There the prophet Daniel caught a glimpse of the battle between good and evil supernatural powers (see Dan. 10:13).

Daniel had been praying for Jerusalem. He learned from the writings of Jeremiah the prophet that Jerusalem must lie desolate for 70 years; that God would not allow His captive people to return to their land for 70 years (see Jer. 25:11-12; 29:10). Daniel pleaded with God to bring about the promised return of His people to their land. He had read Jeremiah's prophecy and knew that this 70-year period was coming to an end. In response, God sent a heavenly messenger with a word about the future. Although God sent a messenger to Daniel, powerful obstacles detained him for three weeks. Still, Daniel faithfully continued praying and fasting, and eventually God's messenger arrived.

The answers to our prayers may likewise be hindered by unseen obstacles. As believers, we should not expect God's answers to come too easily or too quickly. Prayer may be challenged by evil forces, so when we pray we must do so fervently and earnestly. Then we must expect God to answer in His good timing.

The spirit world is real! Yet what a comfort it is to know that God is sovereign. He was in control in Jerusalem in

Daniel's day and He has been moving in history, controlling the destinies of people, ever since. Despite news reports or personal battles, we can be confident that God is in control.

Every human being is influenced by both realms—spiritual and natural. That which is flesh is flesh, and that which is spirit is spirit. Flesh can never be spirit and spirit can never be flesh. Yet spirit dwells in flesh. Our bodies are temples of the Holy Spirit, and flesh can be in the spirit (see 1 Cor. 3:16-17). Whenever a person completely yields his spirit, soul, and body to God or satan, dynamic supernatural power is demonstrated. The Bible assures us, however, that complete deliverance from satanic oppression is available to all believers. Deliverance is planned, purchased, promised, provided, and practiced.

1. *Deliverance Planned*
   Before the foundation of the world, God planned and purposed that His Church would be holy, consecrated and set apart for Him, and blameless in His sight. God planned total freedom for mankind.

According as He hath chosen us in Him before the foundation of the world, that we should be holy and without blame before Him in love (Ephesians 1:4).

2. *Deliverance Purchased*
   Jesus Christ brought deliverance through His death and the shedding of His precious blood. His resurrection completed this eternal transaction. Jesus gave Himself for us that He might deliver us from this present evil world.

Who gave Himself for our sins, that He might deliver us from this present evil world, according to the will of God and our Father (Galatians 1:4).

And they overcame him [satan] *by the blood of the Lamb, and by the word of their testimony...* (Revelation 12:11).

3. *Deliverance Promised*

If the Word of God has not set the basis for deliverance, then there is no basis. God's Word promises freedom for all who believe. He promised to answer our prayer when we ask Him to "deliver us from evil."

And the Lord shall deliver me from every evil work, and will preserve me unto His heavenly kingdom: to whom be glory for ever and ever. Amen (2 Timothy 4:18).

And it shall come to pass, that whosoever shall call on the name of the Lord shall be delivered: for in mount Zion and in Jerusalem shall be deliverance, as the Lord hath said, and in the remnant whom the Lord shall call (Joel 2:32).

And ye shall know the truth, and the truth shall make you free (John 8:32).

He sent His word, and healed them, and delivered them from their destructions (Psalm 107:20).

And these signs shall follow them that believe; In My name shall they cast out devils... (Mark 16:17).

4. *Deliverance Provided*

God has provided a way out of the realm of darkness. This way is through Jesus Christ. Even death is no longer a source of dread or fear. Christ overcame death and one day all believers will as well. Death has been defeated, and we have hope beyond the grave.

Who hath delivered us from the power of darkness, and hath translated us into the kingdom of His dear Son (Colossians 1:13).

O death, where is thy sting? O grave, where is thy victory? ... But thanks be to God, which giveth us the victory through our Lord Jesus Christ (1 Corinthians 15:55,57).

5. *Deliverance Practiced*

The anointing of the Holy Spirit empowers every believer. The anointing upon Jesus Christ and upon His believers, who in faith appropriate His provisions, makes deliverance possible. Luke 4:18 describes five classes of people that may receive deliverance: the broken, brokenhearted, bound, blind, and bruised.

When the enemy shall come in like a flood, the Spirit of the Lord shall lift up a standard against him (Isaiah 59:19b).

The Spirit of the Lord is upon Me, because He hath anointed Me to preach the gospel to the poor; He hath sent Me to heal the brokenhearted, to preach deliverance to the captives, and recovering of sight to the blind, to set at liberty them that are bruised (Luke 4:18).

Jesus: The Great Deliverer

Throughout Jesus' earthly ministry, He gave evidence that spiritual evil power was behind visible evil acts. Over one-fourth of His ministry involved casting out evil spirits.

Acts 10:38	God anointed Jesus to heal all who were oppressed by the devil.
Matthew 12:28	The Kingdom of God comes to you when evil spirits go.
Matthew 8:16-17	Jesus drove out spirits with a word and restored to health the people He set free.
Matthew 9:32-33	A dumb man spoke and multitudes marveled when the devil was cast out.

Matthew 8:14-15	Fever left Peter's mother-in-law when Jesus rebuked the spirit.
Luke 13:11-13	A woman bowed over for 18 years was made straight when loosed from the spirit of infirmity.
Matthew 17:14-18	An epileptic child was delivered by Jesus when His disciples failed.
Mark 7:25-30	The Syrophenician woman's daughter, who was grievously vexed, was made whole the same hour.
Matthew 8:26	A storm stopped when Jesus rebuked the unseen controlling spirit.
Mark 8:33	Satan was rebuked when he inspired Peter's words and thoughts.
Mark 1:23-26	The unclean spirit in the man in the temple came out by Jesus' command.
Matthew 8:28-32	Two men in the country of the Gergesenes who were possessed with demons were freed. The evil spirits were cast into a herd of swine.
Mark 9:38-39	Jesus spoke of the casting out of devils as a miracle.

Full-Benefit Coverage

Does God protect the believer from satan's power? Yes, but He does so conditionally. God has limited satan's power and has provided security for His children. However, it is faith in the benefits of Jesus Christ's redemptive works and obedience to God's commands, that grants "full-benefit coverage." We must act on God's Word and cooperate with God's power.

Some things God does *for us*, but other things require a "co-laborer with God" policy.

A Christian can be sincere but ignorant. Ignorance of the truth, as previously stated, opens the door to deception. When God's laws are broken, sometimes the consequences are not altered. Consider the deliverance of the children of Israel from bondage in Egypt (see Ex. 12). They not only applied the lamb's blood to the doorpost, as instructed by Moses and Aaron, which caused the death angel to pass by, but they also remained inside the house. Otherwise they too would have been at the mercy of the death angel. It was important for the children of Israel to follow God's instructions completely in order for their deliverance to be sure and thorough. There was no guarantee of protection if they did not remain in the house.

Matthew 12:43-45 teaches that a person's condition becomes worse if he gains but fails to maintain freedom from evil spirits. Simply cleaning up one's life without filling it with God leaves plenty of room for satan to reenter. Unless a person sincerely desires to live for Christ, the results of deliverance ministry seem temporary. The Book of Ezra records how the people of Israel rid themselves of idolatry, but failed to replace it with love and obedience to God. Thus wanting to rid our lives of sin is the first step—then we must fill our lives with God's Word and the Holy Spirit.

Maintaining Your Deliverance

Once an individual accepts Jesus Christ as Lord and Savior and is saved, this new believer has the personal responsibility of maintaining his deliverance by cultivating a life of consistent growth in the things of God. Accepting Christ is instantaneous. However, it takes time, effort, and discipline on your part to become a mature and powerful believer. In order to maintain your deliverance you must cultivate:

1. *Your personal prayer life.* Find a private place and set up a daily time for talking with God. Keep a list of persons and situations you want to pray about. Instead of always asking God for things in prayer, learn to praise and thank Him for past answers.

2. *God-consciousness.* Try to constantly center your thoughts on God and scriptural truth. Doing so will crowd out wrong thinking and empower you during moments of weakness and strong temptations. Memorize Scripture verses that give you encouragement during difficult times. Carry a pocket Bible and read it.

3. *Your daily Bible-reading habit.* Establish a place, time, and system for Bible study. Early morning is often the best time because then you have placed *mind-pictures* of truth into your spirit for the rest of the day. Make notes in your Bible that help you. Don't miss a single day.

4. *Godly relationships.* Be very selective when choosing friends. Friends will *add to* or *take away* from your life. Proverbs 13:20 says, "He that walketh with wise men shall be wise: but a companion of fools shall be destroyed."

5. *A teachable spirit.* We must be willing to receive correction and instruction from those who are more spiritually mature. Through instruction and even criticism, we grow in grace and humility. Proverbs 1:5 says that "a wise man will hear," and Proverbs 1:7 says, "The fear of the Lord is the beginning of knowledge: but fools despise wisdom and instruction."

6. *A godly attitude.* View every day as a gift from God. Think good things about yourself and others. Resist complaining. Project enthusiasm. Talk positive words. Stop thinking about obstacles and start thinking about

your opportunities. Avoid negative and depressing conversations.

Growth Inhibitors

Recently I planted a garden of beautiful, colorful flowers in my backyard. One day I was admiring their fresh spring beauty and noticed a few weeds that had grown up around them. Just as weeds choke out the life of a beautiful flower, so there are things in the life of every believer that must be removed in order for the believer to grow. To ensure consistent, unhindered growth, you must eliminate these *"spiritual weeds"* from your life.

1. *Bitterness and unforgiveness.* In Ephesians 4:31 Paul tells us, "Let all bitterness, and wrath, and anger, and clamour, and evil speaking, be put away from you...." Bitterness is like a cancerous sore that spreads its deterioration throughout the inward soul of a person. Forgive those who have hurt you. Repent of your unforgiveness and ask God to pour out His love through you to others.

2. *Wrong relationships.* Distance yourself from ungodly people. Get rid of anything that clouds your mind or spirit. Ask yourself, "Will this friendship bring me closer to Jesus, or will it soil the beauty of what God has begun in me?"

3. *Moral impurity.* Nothing can destroy your testimony and inner joy faster than immorality. When satan plants the "seed" of an immoral thought in your mind, immediately resist it. Exercise your authority. Say, "Satan, I bind you and resist your ungodly suggestion. I am a child of God walking in the power of the Holy Spirit. I give your thought back to you. I am a new creature in

Jesus." Then immediately thank God aloud for good, wholesome, godly thoughts.

4. *Ungodly mind-manipulators.* We are greatly influenced by what we see and hear. Sensual movies and music and suggestive reading material guarantee spiritual suicide. Remove these influences by saturating your life and home environment with wholesome books, tapes, and Christian material.

5. *Time wasters.* Chart your course hourly, daily, and monthly. Set goals and stay on target. God is a planner. From the creation of a world in seven days to a scheduled rapture, it is easy to conclude that our God is a Master in planning details and setting goals, priorities, and order. Learn to avoid nonessentials and energy wasters. Make your time count.

Lastly, not only do you need to put time, effort, and discipline into becoming a mature believer and maintaining your deliverance from the oppression of satan, but you also must set apart or dedicate to God certain areas of your life. Three areas of your life must be consecrated to God:

1. *Your talents and abilities.* Every individual is born with God-given gifts and abilities. It is up to you to discover and develop what God has given to you. *You* are responsible for *you.* Whether you possess genius in music, speaking, mechanics, sports, management, or volunteer work in a ministry, you are here on purpose. Be the best at what you do. Don't just put God in first place; put Him *every* place. "Whatsoever ye do, do all to the glory of God" (1 Cor. 10:31b).

2. *Your job and career.* God wants you to feel happy and fulfilled in your job. If you are not excited about going to work each day, something is wrong. Many people

are trapped in undesirable careers through fear—fear of failure or fear of the unknown. Invest time in learning more about your field. If you feel dissatisfied and unfulfilled in your work, seek God's guidance concerning a new direction or new career, then learn more about other fields. Information breeds motivation. Dare to step up and out into new opportunities. Since we invest so much time in our career or at our place of employment, this must be an area where God can use us.

3. *Your money.* Money is important. Jesus talked about it, and the apostle Paul talked about it. Money also talks; it reveals your true values. It is the power part of you. With it you bargain and exchange your way through life. It helps you acquire your food, your shelter, and your clothing. What you do with your money is important to God. Abraham gave ten percent to God in thanksgiving for His blessing. In Matthew 23:23 Jesus even commended the Pharisees for giving ten percent. Tithing and giving offerings to God is not the payment of a debt to God—all of it belongs to Him. Tithing is the *acknowledgment* of the debt. Financial gifts to God are seeds planted in holy soil, and He personally guarantees a bountiful return.

Authority and Peace

To wage effective spiritual warfare and *crash satan's party*, we must understand spiritual authority. Spiritual authority is not forcing your will upon another. When you have spiritual authority, you establish God's peace in an area that was once full of conflict and oppression. The apostle Paul taught, "And the God of peace shall bruise Satan under your feet shortly" (Rom. 16:20a). When we maintain peace during warfare, it serves as a crushing death blow to satanic oppression and fear. Our victory comes through refusing to judge by what our eyes see or our ears hear, and by trusting that what God has promised will come to pass.

In the battles of life, your peace is actually a weapon. Your confidence in what God has promised you declares to the devil that you are not falling for his lies. Thus the first step toward having spiritual authority over satan is having peace in spite of your circumstances. Whenever Jesus confronted the devil, He did not do so with His emotions or in fear. Knowing that the devil is a liar, Jesus simply refused to be influenced by any other voice than God's.

Satan's arsenal contains such things as fear, worry, doubt, self-pity, and anger. Every one of these weapons robs you of peace and leaves you troubled inside. Do you want to discern where the enemy is coming against you? In the network of your relationships, wherever you do not have peace, you have war. Conversely, wherever you have victory, you have peace. Therefore the more peace you have during adversity, when satan hurls his darts against you, the more you are walking in Christ's victory.

Our peace, our immovable stand upon the Word of God, is a sign that we are positioned correctly in perfect submission to the will of God. Paul tells us to be in no way alarmed or disturbed by our opponents, for it is a sign of destruction for them, but of salvation for us.

And in nothing terrified by your adversaries: which is to them an evident token of perdition, but to you of salvation, and that of God (Philippians 1:28).

The very fact that you are in no way alarmed by your adversary is a sign that you have authority over him.

Protection

When we allow God to guide us and protect us, we have contentment. In Psalm 23 God is seen as a caring and dependable guide. He is our only hope for security in this life.

In Middle Eastern culture, it was customary to anoint a guest at a banquet with fragrant oil. The host of the banquet also was expected to protect his guests at all costs. God offers you the protection of a host even when enemies surround you. Because God is with you, every adversity you face will turn into victory as you maintain your faith in God. The battle you are in will soon become as a meal to you; it will become an experience that will nourish and build you up spiritually.

Thou preparest a table before me in the presence of mine enemies: Thou anointest my head with oil; my cup runneth over (Psalm 23:5).

When describing the Lord as a shepherd, David wrote out of his own experience, from the early years he had spent caring for sheep (see 1 Sam. 16:10-11). Sheep are completely dependent on their shepherd for provision, guidance, and protection. Sheep tend to go astray (see Is. 53:6). They need to be led and guided to places where they can pasture and rest (see Num. 27:17). But sheep also were the wealth of Israel. In spite of their weaknesses, they were precious, and shepherds dedicated a lifetime to their care.

As a good shepherd, Jesus cares first of all for His sheep. Satan, the thief, seeks to steal and kill. So as a good shepherd, Jesus laid down His life for the sheep. (See John 10:11,14.) There is an intimate relationship between Jesus and His sheep, to whom He gives life to the full (see Jn. 10,14). Those who are truly sheep recognize their Shepherd's voice.

The New Testament calls Jesus the Good Shepherd (see Jn. 10:11); the Great Shepherd (see Heb. 13:20-21); and the Head Shepherd (see 1 Pet. 5:4). As the Lord is the Good Shepherd, so we are His sheep. We are not His sheep in the sense that we are dumb, frightened, passive animals, but as obedient followers wise enough to follow One who will lead us to right places and in right ways. The Psalmist David does not focus on the animal-like qualities of sheep, but on the discipleship qualities of those who follow. Even death is not a threat to those who follow Christ.

Death casts the most frightening shadow of all over our lives because we are the most helpless in its presence. We can struggle with many other enemies—pain, suffering, disease, and injury—but we cannot wrestle with death. Death is a deadly opponent. It has the final word. Only one Person can walk with us through death's dark valley and bring us through safely to the other side—the God of life, our Shepherd, our Lord. When we allow God our Shepherd to guide us, we have contentment.

Fake It Till You Make It

As a believer, I realize that the struggles many of us still encounter in our day-to-day existence are agonizing and tormenting. Maintaining our deliverance from the oppression of satan is a daily effort. This Christian life can be very difficult at times to be sure, for we live in a fallen world. But the Word of God assures us that the power to overcome is always present with us. We are never alone. When Jesus was about to face the persecution of the cross of Calvary, He prophesied that His most intimate companions and friends would desert Him. "And yet," He said, "I am not alone, because the Father is with Me" (Jn. 16:32). As we struggle, we need to remind ourselves of two things that Jesus said in John 16:33:

1. We would have tribulation.
2. We would overcome.

Even though we don't always "feel like" we are overcoming, we can look beyond our present circumstances to what God has promised "will be." See yourself *set free*; picture yourself *delivered* from all oppression.

When I was six years old, which was quite some time ago, I was a very shy, reserved little girl in school. Because of my shyness and insecurity, I was gripped with fear every time I had to speak or read aloud in front of the class. I was a very good reader, so the teacher often called on me. Every time I was called upon to read, my hands would get sweaty, my knees would knock, my face would pale, and I would drop my book or stumble over my feet getting to the front of the classroom. The other students knew of the anxiety I felt because my fear was manifested in my behavior. Then one day in music class I learned the words to a song that are forever etched in my brain. I don't remember the words of the verses or the song's title, but for years, whenever I encountered a stressful situation, I would whisper the chorus of that little song:

> Whenever I feel afraid
> I hold my head erect
> And whistle a happy tune
> So no one will suspect, I'm afraid.

> While trembling in my shoes
> I strike a careless pose
> And whistle a happy tune
> So no one ever knows, I'm afraid.

Fear still gripped me at times, but no one suspected my true feelings because my behavior did not reflect my fear. In time I gained the self-confidence I needed to overcome my anxiety. I learned to "fake it till you make it."

Reacting to a negative situation with a positive attitude is a demonstration of faith. As believers we must "act like" we have victory in all situations because by faith we believe what God has promised. Fear is not from God, so the feelings of fear over what satan is trying to do in our life are themselves part of satan's oppression.

For God hath not given us the spirit of fear; but of power, and of love, and of a sound mind (2 Timothy 1:7).

Never allow fear to get the better of you. Never let evil get the better of you. Instead, get the better of evil by thinking and doing good (see Rom. 12:21). Learn to encourage yourself daily with some healthy "self-talk":

- I am delivered from _____.
- I am set free from satan's oppression.
- I am a new creature in Christ.
- I do have victory over _____.
- God is with me.
- I have God's love, God's power, and a sound mind.

Rest and Rule

Only God's peace will quell our fleshly reactions to satanic oppression. The source of God's peace is God Himself. In Psalm 23 David declares, "Yea, though I walk through the valley of the shadow of death, I will fear no evil: for Thou art with me..." (verse 4). There is a place of walking with God where we simply fear no evil. The Lord knows the "green pastures" and "still waters" that will restore us and give us rest and peace (see Ps. 23:2-3). David faced a lion, a bear, and a giant, yet he feared no evil (see 1 Sam. 17:34-37). David's trust and confidence was in the Lord.

God is our source of rest and peace. Revelation 4:6 assures us, "And before the throne there was a sea of glass like unto crystal...." The glass sea is a symbol. It shows there are no ripples, no waves, no anxieties troubling God. God is never worried. He is never in a hurry, nor ever without an answer. The sea around Him is perfectly still and totally calm. All our victories flow out from being seated there with Him.

Before you go into warfare, recognize that it is not you whom the devil is afraid of—it is *Christ in you*. God says to all believers, "Sit at My right hand until I make your enemies a footstool" (see Ps. 110:1). Position yourself in the presence of God. Sit at rest in the knowledge that Christ has already made your enemies a footstool for your feet.

Rest precedes rule and peace precedes power. Do not seek to rule over satan until you submit to God's rule over you. The focus of all victory comes from seeking God and then allowing His presence to fill your spirit with His peace. To maintain your deliverance from satanic oppression, pray this prayer:

Lord, give me the discipline I need to cultivate a life of consistent growth in You. Grant me discernment to see the subtlety of satan as he works to oppress my life. Give me a teachable spirit so I can receive correction and instruction from You. Eliminate the "spiritual weeds" that hinder my growth. Make my enemies my footstool, and deliver me from all evil.

Chapter 8

THE PARTY'S OVER

*And we know that all things work together
for good to them that love God, to them
who are the called according to His purpose.*
Romans 8:28

W HAT A COMFORT it is to know that God is sovereign in all things. In spite of satan's power, his final destiny is fixed. Jesus Christ crashed satan's party at Calvary. The victory over sin and death was sealed. As believers, we are overcomers. God promises us that even our mistakes and wrong choices will work together for our good.

God's highest purpose is not for you to constantly bind satan in your life; rather, He wants to teach you how to become an overcomer. You must participate in this. Positive action is required. As you discover and implement this action in your life, you can *pull the plug* on the downfall satan has planned for you.

Jesus Says "Come to Me"

The first step in becoming an overcomer is to come to Jesus and stay attached to Him. Matthew 11:28-30 says:

Come unto Me, all ye that labour and are heavy laden, and I will give you rest. Take My yoke upon you, and learn of Me; for I am meek and lowly in heart: and ye shall find rest unto your souls. For My yoke is easy, and My burden is light (Matthew 11:28-30).

Even though we are saved, filled with the Holy Ghost, and believe in the miracle-working power of God, situations arise that cause us to realize that life is often an intense struggle.

Something needs to be understood. Satan is not trying to *steal* your salvation. He knows that he cannot. That is an impossibility. Once you accept Jesus Christ as Lord and Savior, you are not in danger of losing your salvation to another person or power. If such a thing were possible, that power would be greater than the keeping power of God. We do not need to live life in fear and trembling wondering, *Will this be the day?* or *Will this be the situation?* that causes God to be an "Indian giver" and take back His redemption as an act of retribution. John 10:28-29 says:

And I give unto them eternal life; and they shall never perish, neither shall any man pluck them out of My hand. My Father, which gave them Me, is greater than all; and no man is able to pluck them out of My Father's hand (John 10:28-29).

God our Father is greater than the united forces of all our enemies, natural and supernatural. So no one need fear being snatched out of God's hands. The only thing one must do is to come to God and permit His saving and keeping power to be manifested. However, God will not keep one contrary to his or her will any more than He kept lucifer, the fallen angels, pre-Adamites, Adam and Eve, and many others who willed to sin.

Although Satan cannot cause you to lose your salvation, he can, with your cooperation, cause your downfall and hinder the power of God in your life. However, Jesus provided a way for everyone who labors in these battles. In order to defeat satan's plan, you must:

1. Accept Jesus' invitation to "Come."
2. Cast your cares upon Him.
3. Take His yoke upon you.
4. Surrender to Him.

Accept Jesus' Invitation to Come

When you face difficulties in your life, you do not have to look to your own ability, your own reasoning, or your own plans and purposes. You can come to Jesus and stay attached to Him. You simply need to accept His invitation.

Even though Jesus lives in you, perhaps you have not released yourself to Him completely. Are you still holding on to your own plans and your own agenda? Do you want to do things your way and not His? If you continue in that mindset, you are taking on burdens and cares that you were not meant to carry. Jesus is the one the prophet Isaiah spoke of: "Surely He hath borne our griefs, and carried our sorrows" (Is. 53:4a).

Jesus was a man of sorrows because He carried our sorrow. He personally had no sin, sickness, pain, or suffering as a result of His own life. However, we have these in abundance, and Jesus came into the world to carry them for us. He became identified with our sufferings by taking them upon Himself and bearing them unto death so that we might be free from them.

The Hebrew word *choliy* (translated "grief") means "malady, weaknesses, sicknesses, diseases, infirmities, anxieties, and calamities." To *carry* means "to bear or convey as a penalty." Jesus bore our sufferings so that we would not have to. Accept His invitation to "Come."

Cast Your Cares Upon Him

Are you burdened with sickness, family problems, or business problems? Do you have emotional, mental, or spiritual problems? Satan celebrates when your mind is so confused that you do not know what to do.

Jesus said through Peter in First Peter 5:7, "Casting all your care upon Him; for He careth for you." In other words, Jesus says, "Stop trying to fix it yourself!" Stop looking to the world for the answer. The world's system and God's system are completely different. John 15:19 says, "If ye were of the world...therefore the world hateth you."

We are on foreign territory here. We do not really belong to this world. We belong to Jesus because we have been born from above. Therefore, we must stop struggling to survive the world's way. Jesus said, "He that findeth his life shall lose it: and he that loseth his life for My sake shall find it" (Mt. 10:39).

The thing that is crushing the very life out of you may not be the problem you face, but that you are trying to fix it yourself. You may be still holding on to your program, your agenda, your will, and your life. Jesus said, "He that loseth his life for My sake shall find it." Instead of surrendering our life to His, we constantly make excuses like, "I'm not ready yet" or "I'm afraid of losing control." As we do this continually, our burdens and problems become more than we can bear.

Take His Yoke Upon You

Do you know what a *yoke* is? A *yoke* is "a contrivance for fastening the necks of two animals together for work." Years ago a yoke or collar went over the neck of each animal and linked them together. Many times the farmer yoked up an experienced ox to a young ox so the older one could train him. If the young ox tried to go in another direction (other than where the older ox was headed), the yoke stopped him. The young ox began to understand that he was not going to go anywhere or do anything on his own. The experienced ox was the leader and the young ox followed his lead. Before long, this very young, inexperienced, know-it-all, wanting-its-own-way ox got the message. Does this sound familiar?

This same principle works for us. Jesus said in Matthew 11:29-30 "Take My yoke upon you, and learn of Me; for...My yoke is easy, and My burden is light." We must learn to *move* when Jesus *moves*. How many of us have felt like saying, "*God, You are too slow...I need an answer now*"? So we take the situation into our own hands, move ahead of God, and end up in a mess.

Sometimes we may want to say, "*Lord, I'm tired. I'm just going to do nothing for awhile*," but Jesus has other plans. He begins to tug and pull, moving us in a new direction. If we do not choose God's will and move with Him, then the pressure of the yoke comes upon us. We cannot pull Jesus in the opposite direction.

Then there are times that we feel like making a change and all of a sudden we experience a great tug again. Why? It is because we are yoked up with Jesus and He is not ready to make a change. He is headed straight ahead. The key to God's rest, even with burdens and cares, is learning to move when Jesus moves and to turn or stop as He directs. How do we do that? We simply need to surrender!

Surrender to Him

Each day we must surrender a little more of *self* to a little more of Jesus. This comes from a desire for a deeper relationship with Him. By reading and studying the Word of God diligently, we begin to understand what He expects of us. We learn to hear His *still small voice* when we spend precious moments in silence and prayer before Him.

It is so wonderful to be yoked up with the One who paid the price for your sins and mine at Calvary. Jesus wants you to feel His peace in every situation. He wants you to be assured of His faithfulness, even in the face of adversity. Jesus wants you to be at peace as He leads and directs your life. He wants you to trust Him completely in every situation.

Satan will try to convince you that nothing is changing. Then, you begin to think, *I must take charge...I must do it my way.* Read Romans 10:9. To "believe with the heart" means to trust in, rely upon, and adhere to His lordship in your life. When we confess Him as Lord, we openly profess our complete dependence on Him. Believing with your heart yokes your self to Him. This means that you are determined to go where He wants you to go and do what He wants you to do because you are no longer trusting in *self.*

Pulling the Plug

When I was a teenager, my friends and I used to go to house parties. House parties were gatherings of young people and usually held in someone's basement, backyard, or garage. We would get together to dance, socialize, and check each other out in the hope of finding a new "squeeze." The lights were low, and the music was mellow. The pungent smell of cheap cologne and tacky perfume punctuated the atmosphere of the room. All you could hear was the shuffle of feet dancing to the measured beat of a "slow drag."

Then it happened. The high pitched harmony of the "do wop group" got slower and slower and slower. What happened...was the world coming to an end? Almost...somebody had pulled the plug. The worst thing that could happen at a house party was to have someone disconnect the source that provided the music.

Maybe the chaperons did it because the hour was getting late. Or perhaps some unwanted guests were trying to cause trouble. It did not matter. Pulling the plug meant one thing—the party's over. Not one word had to be said. The sigh of disappointment rang out like a funeral dirge in the dimly lit, overheated room. No explanations had to be offered. When the party was over, it was over.

Immediately the bright lights were turned on. Everyone squinted as their eyes adjusted to the light, hastily reaching for hats and coats in preparation to leave. The party was over!

Skeletons in Your Closet

You can crash the devil's party. You can pull the plug and disconnect the source that keeps you defeated and in bondage. Every yoke of bondage that has kept you feeling defeated can be broken. Christians often say that "the anointing breaks the yoke." However, the Word of God says, "...and the yoke shall be destroyed because of the anointing" (Is. 10:27).

The key word in this verse is *destroyed*. Many people have their yokes merely *broken* and not destroyed. Broken yokes can be repaired, mended, and resurrected. Every sin, problem, and form of degradation that once burdened us and hindered our progress in God can be picked up again.

I see this so often as a pastor. People are unable to move forward in God because of a *past* that plagues them. God readily forgives a truly repentant heart, but we often have great difficulty, almost an inability, to forgive ourselves.

The blood of Jesus is so potent and so powerful that it can penetrate through years of sin and degradation. There are no skeletons in your closet. If you hear the bones of your past rattling, you are listening to sounds that you have put there. Your closet has been cleaned out.

If you have committed fornication, adultery, or prostitution, *God has forgiven you*.

If you have abused alcohol or drugs, *God has forgiven you*.

If you have experienced divorce or a failed relationship, *God has forgiven you*.

If you have committed murder by taking someone's life or by having an abortion, *God has forgiven you*.

You, yourself, must silence the rattling of every skeleton in your spiritual closet. You do this by:

1. Asking and receiving God's forgiveness.
2. Forgiving yourself.
3. Forgiving others.
4. Proclaiming "*God has forgiven me!*"

A New Nature

Before we believed in Christ, our nature was evil. We disobeyed, rebelled, and ignored God. Even at our best we still fall short of loving God with all our heart, soul, and spirit. However, those of us who have accepted Christ as Lord and Savior have a new nature. God has crucified the old rebellious nature.

Knowing this, that our old man is crucified with Him, that the body of sin might be destroyed, that henceforth we should not serve sin (Romans 6:6).

The "old man" that Paul refers to is the old sin nature. Expressions such as: "dead to sin," "crucified with Him," "dead with Christ," and "dead to the law" were common among

Hebrews, Greeks, Romans, and other people. *To die to a thing or person* means "to have nothing to do with it and to be totally separated from it or him." *To live to a person or a thing* is "to be wholly given up to and to have an intimate connection with that person or thing." Crucifying the old man means that you have no further dealing with the sin nature. Born-again believers are free from sin and satan.

> *We know that whosoever is born of God sinneth not; but he that is begotten of God keepeth himself, and that wicked one toucheth him not* (1 John 5:18).

Christ came to take away our sins, and if we still have them, it is proof that we have not truly repented of them. We are born of God when the Holy Spirit lives in us and gives us Jesus' new life. Being *born again* is more than a "fresh start," it is a "rebirth." The Holy Spirit gives us a new mind and a new heart to make the "God choice" in our decisions and behavior. The Holy Spirit, living in us, enables us to be like Christ. Our perspective changes too. Our mind and thinking pattern is renewed every day by the Holy Spirit, so we begin to think and act differently.

Party Poopers

We all have areas in our life where temptation is strong and habits are difficult to conquer. These weaknesses give satan a foothold in our life, so we must deal with them. The apostle John says something that seems shocking:

> *He that committeth sin is of the devil; for the devil sinneth from the beginning...Whosoever is born of God doth not commit sin; for His seed remaineth in him: and he cannot sin, because he is born of God* (1 John 3:8-9).

John is not talking about people whose victories are still incomplete. He is talking about people who make a practice of sinning and look for ways to justify it. Those who have been born of God do not sin because God's seed abides in them. By "God's seed abides in them" John refers to "true believers who do not make a practice of sinning, nor become indifferent to God's moral law."

All believers still sin, but they should be working for victory over sin. Satan delights in our failure to overcome sin. However, his party is over when we learn how to crash his party and defeat his wicked plan for our life. Three steps are necessary to find victory over prevailing sin:

1. Seek the power of the Holy Spirit and God's Word.
2. Stay away from tempting situations.
3. Seek the help of the Body of Christ—their accountability and prayers.

The Christian life is a process of becoming more and more like Christ. This process will not be complete until we see Christ face-to-face, but knowing our ultimate goal should motivate us to purify ourselves. To *purify* means "to keep morally straight, free from corruption of sin."

God also purifies us, but we must take action to remain morally fit. Yokes should be destroyed, not temporarily dismantled. The anointing, which is the power and presence of God, is obtained by living a consecrated life of fasting, prayer, and reading God's Word. Although it is God's responsibility to set you free, there are some things that you must do to get rid of the skeletons in your closed and remain free:

1. Forgive
2. Forget
3. Fellowship

You must forgive yourself and any person or persons who have offended or violated you in the past. As awful as it may have been, you cannot change your past. You cannot think it away, pray it away, or wish it away. It is what it was, but with the help of the Holy Spirit you can reshape your future by forgiving those who have wronged you. Unforgiveness hinders the flow of God in your life. It is an unnecessary weight that can "so easily beset you." (See Hebrews 12:1.)

The Christian life involves hard work. Yet, in our struggles against sin we do not have to "go it alone." In fact, we are not capable of successfully overcoming sin in our lives. If we could, there would be no need for the keeping power of the Holy Spirit. To "crash satan's party" in your life, pray this believer's prayer:

Lord, I thank You for Your keeping power. Help me to remember that I have victory over every area of my life. All I have to do is to ask. I cast my every care upon You. Help me to forgive those who have hurt me in the past. Help me to love others unconditionally as Christ also loved and forgave me. Amen.

Chapter 9

THE FINAL CELEBRATION

*And after these things I heard a great voice
of much people in heaven, saying, Alleluia; Salvation,
and glory, and honour, and power, unto the Lord our God.*
Revelation 19:1

I'VE MET the enemy! I have looked him and his demons square in the face and crashed his party. I have become an expert in dealing with the enemy. I know how to use the power God has given me to successfully destroy his works. When satan attacked every area of my life, I knew how to successfully destroy his works. I have learned how to take authority over him and to use the power that God has given me.

Sometimes I felt silly shouting loudly and I know I looked strange rebuking demons that no one else could see, but I knew they were there. I took authority over every demonic force and satan himself—and it worked!

Satan had an open invitation with my name on it; however, I crashed his party. I pulled the plug on his plans for my life, and when I did I slept like a baby all night, for the first time in a year, and my home was at peace.

My test *was not* over. My trials *had not* ended. My storms *had not* abated, but the evil influences that had tormented my life and my home were gone. Satan's party was over.

I know what it means to *resist the devil*. I know what it means to be an overcomer. I put what I learned from God's Word into practice in my life, and to my delight, it worked! Every time I drew close to the Lord I pulled the plug on satan's plans and crashed his party.

An Extensive Guest List

Satan seeks out those who are weak, indecisive, and unstable in their walk with the Lord. He is never relaxed. He is continually, plotting, planning, scheming, and scheduling his malicious activities. Satan harasses new converts with doubt and confusion. He torments growing saints with fear and trepidation. He tortures mature saints with worry and frustration.

He has a plan for every believer and when we succumb to his tactics, he puts us on his guest list. When he sees you falling in sin, he starts to prepare for the party and his decor is always the same—darkness. He issued his first invitation in the Garden of Eden when he tempted Adam and Eve to sin (see Gen. 3:4), and he has been writing invitations ever since.

Mission Possible

Every day that we walk in our new nature is a day that satan loses more and more ground, and he does not like that. The devil knows that he has lost your soul to Christ. However, his evil is total, so he will try to manipulate your walk in the Lord.

The truth is, you have been crucified with Christ. Your old nature died when you were born again. Nevertheless you live, but it is not you, at least not the old you. Now it is Christ who lives in you. He has become your life. The life you now live in the flesh is one of faith in Christ, who loved us, and has made it possible for us to live by faith.

I am crucified with Christ: nevertheless I live; yet not I, but Christ liveth in me: and the life which I now live in the flesh I live by the faith of the Son of God, who loved me, and gave Himself for me (Galatians 2:20).

The Bible is true. You did die with Christ. The only thing you must do is lay aside the old self. Holding on to vestiges of the old nature gives satan opportunity to cause trouble in your life. You are not two people. You do not have a "good" you and a "bad" you. It is true that the spirit and flesh wage war with each other, but there is only one *you*. Your true self is in Christ. You are a spirit person.

Our mission then is to walk in this truth. The only way this great truth will become resident in our hearts will be for us to allow our thoughts to be established in the grace of God. Grace is our bulwark against the deceptive snares of the devil.

The Final Blow

When one is born again, one enters the realm of the supernatural and spiritual. A study of the Bible should begin immediately to see what it teaches regarding how one should walk and conduct oneself in spiritual warfare with satan and demons. Saints are to:

1. Put on the whole armor of God (Eph. 6:11-18);
2. Know satan's devices (2 Cor. 2:11);
3. Give him no place (Eph. 4:27);
4. Resist him (Jas. 4:7);
5. Be sober and vigilant lest he devour you (1 Pet. 5:8-9);
6. Overcome him by the Word (Mt. 4:1-11; 1 Jn. 2:14);

7. Overcome him by the blood of Christ and your testimony (Rev. 12:11);
8. Overcome him by Christ and His name (Eph. 1:19-22; 2:6; 2 Cor. 2:14);
9. Overcome him by the birth of the Spirit and in faith (1 Jn. 2:29; 3:9; 5:1-4,18);
10. Overcome him by the Holy Spirit (Rom. 8:1-13; Gal. 5:16-26).

A believer armed with a thorough knowledge of God's Word is a deadly enemy to satan. Satan is "knocked out" before the battle begins. Remember, satan's power is not eternal—he will meet his doom. Although he began his evil work in humankind at the beginning and continues it through today, he will be destroyed when he is thrown into the lake of fire. Satan was forever defeated and humiliated when Christ rose from the grave in glory and power.

The earth as we know it will not last forever. The final crashing will take place when Christ puts down all rebellion in the earth. Satan still exercises great power in the world, but his final destiny is fixed and at that time he will never be a threat to anyone again. When Jesus uttered His final words on the cross, satan's fate was sealed.

> *...that old serpent, called the Devil, and Satan, which deceiveth the whole world: he was cast out into the earth, and his angels were cast out with him* (Revelation 12:9).

When that day comes, the party will be over and satan's season of celebration will come to an end!

What a Party!

In the Book of Revelation, God has a party too. Initial arrangements were made by Christ at Calvary. The formal invitation is found in Romans:

...if thou shalt confess with thy mouth the Lord Jesus, and shalt believe in thine heart that God hath raised Him from the dead, thou shalt be saved (Romans 10:9).

You are invited to the celebration that the Lord gives for His people. We, as believers, go to the celebration through confession and belief in the Lord Jesus Christ.

What shall we wear at the Lord's celebration? It is a "come as you are" affair. It is also a "B.Y.O.B." (bring your own burdens and trade them in for blessings). We shall be clothed in robes of righteousness and crowns of victory. God gives us party favors—love, joy, peace, grace, mercy, forgiveness, and rest.

And God shall wipe away all tears from their eyes; and there shall be no more death, neither sorrow, nor crying, neither shall there be any more pain: for the former things are passed away (Revelation 21:4).

After God's great judgment, He will create a new earth. We do not know *what* the new earth will look like or where it will be, but God and his followers will be united to live there forever.

Have you ever wondered what eternity will be like? The holy city, the new Jerusalem, is described in Revelation 21. It is described as a place where there will be no death, pain, sorrow, or crying. What a wonderful truth!

No matter what you are going through, it is not the last word—God has written the final chapter, and it tells about the true fulfillment and eternal joy for those who love him. We do not know as much as we would like, but we do know enough to see that eternity with God will be more wonderful than we can imagine. What a party! Alleluia!

R.S.V.P.

God gives us all an open invitation to be His eternal guest in glory. Our response to God's invitation is a matter of choice and personal will. Your attendance at the celebration of believers depends upon the decision you make concerning Jesus Christ. The initial request for your attendance has been made at Calvary. Jesus says, "Come." No one can attend both parties. You can only be in one place at one time. You cannot serve both God and satan.

No man can serve two masters: for either he will hate the one, and love the other; or else he will hold to the one, and despise the other. Ye cannot serve God and mammon (Matthew 6:24).

The pathway that leads to God's eternal celebration is narrow. For many, the road is obscured by a willful rejection of Jesus Christ. For others the search is futile because of their love for and preoccupation with sin. Still Jesus says, "Come." The choice is ours.

Spiritual death can be cancelled by repentance. Spiritual life can be cancelled by sin. There is only one way to live eternally with God and only a few decide to follow it:

Enter ye in at the strait gate: for wide is the gate, and broad is the way, that leadeth to destruction, and many there be which go in thereat: Because strait is the gate, and narrow is the way, which leadeth unto life, and few there be that find it (Matthew 7:13-14).

PRAYERS

To Receive Deliverance

Lord, deliver me from sin. Set me free from all bad habits and sinful behavior. Allow my life to be transformed by the work of the Holy Spirit. I desire a new life in Jesus Christ.

To Receive Salvation

Lord, I confess that I am a sinner. I am sorry for my sins and ask your forgiveness. I believe that Jesus paid the penalty for my sins. I receive your gift of mercy and salvation.

To Know God's Word

Lord, help me to know You through Your Word. Bring understanding to my mind and to my heart. Allow Your Word to be put to practical use in my life. Allow Your Word to live in me.

To Clear Away Distraction

Lord help me to focus upon You. I desire to be still before You. Help me to set aside a special time each day where You and I can fellowship together.

To Clean Your Thoughts

Lord, wash away every thought of the world and its agendas and let my mind be at rest. Help me to bring my cares and concerns to You. Unclutter my mind so that I can seek Your will and listen for Your guidance.

To Deepen Your Faith

Lord, I know that faith determines how close I am to You. As my faith increases, so does my confidence and trust that You will meet my needs. Deepen my faith and increase my confidence so that I can learn to lean on You and not on myself.

EPILOGUE

DISCERNMENT IS THE mark of spiritual maturity. Too many Christians choose a gospel message limited to good feelings, comfort, and God's permissive will. Traditions, denominational doctrines, and old religious patterns are comfortable and safe. Few believers press on in their lifestyles into actual Kingdom obedience and spiritual confrontation. Who willingly chooses combat and change? Who willingly gives away securities, social applause, approval, and possessions for a greater cause requiring self-sacrifice?

God's soldiers in the world are those who have ears to hear God's commands. They have the foretaste of the Kingdom of God in their mouths. Kingdom fulfillment is their meat and drink. They are moved to action by God's direction from the Holy Spirit and are easily prompted to do God's will. They are the heros and heroines of a mighty spiritual war. They are the overcomers who will crash satan's party.

Crashing Satan's Party is written to those who have ears to hear what the Spirit of God is saying to the Church in this generation. The Church is responsible to take satan off the throne of worldly kingdoms and put Christ upon it. This is accomplished through an active demonstration of God's alternatives, which offer the world a choice between the kingdoms of darkness and light.

In spiritual battles we no longer rely on any strength of the flesh. We must engage in spiritual warfare inviting heavenly forces to join us. War rages in the heavenlies and human life is a constant struggle. Although all people participate in this struggle regardless of their conscious recognition of it, only God's people can affect the outcome of the warfare intended to defeat the believers in this generation.

Among Christians at all levels of spiritual maturity, God is looking across the earth for people He can trust. The greatest warfare is waged against those who have committed their lives to fully following the Lord. God's chosen people say and do the same things that Jesus' ministry demonstrated. We expose satan and crash his party just as Jesus did (see 1 John 3:8).

No longer do I run to take cover from the enemy. I am not ready prey—nor am I a sitting duck. Some of us accept Jesus as our personal Savior then twiddle our thumbs waiting for the Kingdom to come. This has made some believers very passive. However, we must realize that when Christ was nailed to the cross, He rendered a fatal blow to satan and that the people of God are to arrive on the territory that satan claims is his and crash his party because the Kingdom of Heaven has arrived.

The false view is that the Kingdom is something in the distance and that we must allow evil to prevail in the world until that sudden moment when Christ will appear and rectify everything. Thus satan has cleverly put up "No Trespassing" signs. Wherever he has a "No Trespassing" sign, the people of God have said, "that is off limits because God is in control." Yet Jesus tells us to occupy until He comes (see Lk. 19:13). The word *occupy* is a military word for occupational force. An occupational force is a group of soldiers who slip behind the enemy's line, grab a piece of his territory, claim it, and hold it until the invasion comes.

There is an invasion coming. The kingdoms of this world are going to become the Kingdom of our Lord and of His Christ. He is going to reign forever and ever. But until that time, God's people are to take territory and occupy. The very fact that Paul tells us in Ephesians 6 to "put on the whole armor of God" that we may be able to stand against the insanity of the devil (see Eph. 6:11) is testimony enough that we will be engaged in warfare. We are not to be passive people, twiddling our thumbs waiting for the Kingdom to come. Many people ask me, "Millicent Thompson, don't you believe the Lord is on His way?" "No," I answer quickly, "I *do not* believe the Lord is on His way because it doesn't take Him that long to get here." I do not know about your Scripture, but mine says something about "the twinkling of an eye" (1 Cor. 15:52). Jesus is telling us, "Crash satan's party and occupy till I come!"

Millicent Thompson Ministries
Order Form

PRODUCTS	PRICE	QTY.	AMOUNT
BOOKS			
Crashing Satan's Party	$10.00		
Don't Die in the Winter…Your Season Is Coming!	$10.00		
VIDEOTAPES			
A Ridiculous Blessing	$15.00		
A Treasure in Trash	$15.00		
Back to Your Future	$15.00		
Bent Over in the Synagogue	$15.00		
By Any Means Necessary	$15.00		
Caution! Program Subject to Change	$15.00		
Dead Man Walking	$15.00		
Going Through the Change	$15.00		
If Thou Be a Great People	$15.00		
My Water Just Broke!	$15.00		
Psyche!	$15.00		
Target Practice	$15.00		
The Devil Is Blowing Up Balloons	$15.00		
Weird People	$15.00		
You Got to Be Crazy	$15.00		
Your Attitude Is Showing	$15.00		
Total for books and videotapes			

Millicent Thompson Ministries
Order Form

PRODUCTS	PRICE	QTY.	AMOUNT
AUDIOTAPES			
A Treasure in Trash	$5.00		
Bent Over in the Synagogue	$5.00		
By Any Means Necessary	$5.00		
Don't Die in the Winter…	$5.00		
If Thou Be a Great People	$5.00		
If You Don't Start Nothin', It Ain't Gonna Be Nothin'	$5.00		
It's a Set-up	$5.00		
Let the Daughters Live	$5.00		
My Water Just Broke!	$5.00		
Psyche!	$5.00		
Rally in the Valley	$5.00		
Show Up for the Showdown	$5.00		
Target Practice	$5.00		
This Time I Will Praise the Lord	$5.00		
Waiting to Exhale	$5.00		
Weird People	$5.00		
You Got to Be Crazy	$5.00		
Your Attitude Is Showing	$5.00		
		Subtotal	
Total from books and videotapes			
Add $2.50 for shipping and handling (allow 2-4 weeks for delivery)			
TOTAL AMOUNT ENCLOSED			

Please Print:

Name _____

Address _____

City _____ State _____ Zip _____

Home Phone _____ Daytime Phone _____

Mail to: Millicent Thompson Ministries, Inc., P.O. Box 9143, Philadelphia, PA 19139
Please make checks payable to Millicent Thompson Ministries.
For speaking engagements, please call 610-356-8525.

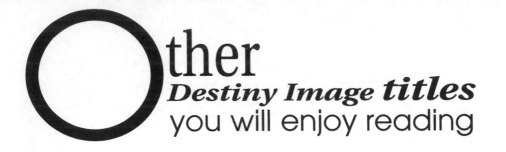

Other

Destiny Image **titles**
you will enjoy reading

DON'T DIE IN THE WINTER...
by Dr. Millicent Thompson.
Why do we go through hard times? Why must we suffer pain? In *Don't Die in the Winter...* Dr. Thompson explains the spiritual seasons and cycles that people experience. A spiritual winter is simply a season that tests our growth. We need to endure our winters, for in the plan of God, spring always follows winter!
Paperback Book, 168p. ISBN 1-56043-558-5 Retail $7.99

THE POWER OF BROKENNESS
by Don Nori.
Accepting Brokenness is a must for becoming a true vessel of the Lord, and is a stepping-stone to revival in our hearts, our homes, and our churches. Brokenness alone brings us to the wonderful revelation of how deep and great our Lord's mercy really is. Join this companion who leads us through the darkest of nights. Discover the *Power of Brokenness*.
Paperback Book, 168p. ISBN 1-56043-178-4 Retail $8.99

I STOOD IN THE FLAMES
by Dr. Wanda A. Davis-Turner.
If you have ever come to a point of depression, fear, or defeat, then you need this book! With honesty, truth, and clarity, Dr. Davis-Turner shares her hard-won principles for victory in the midst of the fire. You can turn satan's attack into a platform of strength and laughter!
Paperback Book, 154p. ISBN 1-56043-275-6 Retail $7.99

WOMAN, THOU ART LOOSED!
by T.D. Jakes.
This book offers healing to hurting single mothers, insecure women, and battered wives; and hope to abused girls and women in crisis! Hurting women around the nation—and those who minister to them—are devouring the compassionate truths in Bishop T.D. Jakes' *Woman, Thou Art Loosed!*
Paperback Book, 210p. ISBN 1-56043-100-8 Retail $9.99

Available at your local Christian bookstore.

Internet: http://www.reapernet.com

Prices subject to change without notice.